IN BLOOM
NOT BROKEN

Katie Maylea

TABLE OF CONTENTS

FOREWORD

In Bloom Not Broken
Sometimes the world seems relentless,
The struggles are endless,
We just seem to battle through,
We think we are helpless,
Destined to wind up friendless,
For others have no clue,
What we forget is this illness
That we have inside us
Is just a small part of you
You are In Bloom Not Broken
So many words unspoken
So many great things to do
You have a world to achieve
If you just believe
That you are okay being you
Don't try to hide
What you have inside
Hold on to what is true.

A BEAUTIFUL STING

I remember the first time I self-harmed. It was odd; I hadn't seen it on the TV – it wasn't broadcasted so openly on programs like it is these days – it wasn't something I'd read about or seen someone else do… I just went into the bathroom feeling like I had so much emotion bubbling inside me that it might actually make me explode; like I needed to rip the house apart brick by brick, needed to tear my own skin off… and I picked up a razor and I cut my arm. It almost didn't hurt. It was a release, a beautiful sting, and watching the blood come out was so satisfying. All that rage and all that hurt came off the boil and just simmered, then it lessened, and finally my head cleared.

Where did it come from? This rage, this emotion? You might as well ask, 'where did I come from?' A lot has been debated about whether mental illness is a result of nature or nurture. Is it something we're born with that comes from our genes, or something that results from our upbringing, from things that happen to us in our childhood? Later, many clinicians would blame my childhood for my mental fragility. But it's true, too, that my mum suffered from aspects of mental illness and I've often wondered if not only I, but my daughter, share traits of her behaviour. All I know for sure is that my brain and my personality did not form in a vacuum. They were the result of my mum, and my dad, and my childhood. And to tell my story, I have to start at the very beginning.

I was due in January of 1986, but I arrived in November of 1985. Impatient from the get-go. Always rushing to get going, regardless of it being a good idea or not. I was whisked away fairly sharply after being born. My parents didn't have much clue as to what was happening and my dad was running around the hospital, shouting and trying to find out what was going on.

I was in the hospital for quite some time and was exceptionally small. My mum bought dolls' clothes to dress me as anything else was just far too big. Apparently, I could fit in my dad's hand. When I finally made it home, I was constantly projectile vomiting and one day, I stopped breathing. I've been told that my lips turned blue, and my dad had me upside down smacking my back to revive me. He once told me that he said, "Don't give her back until she's fixed."

I made it. I survived. I have, however, often wondered whether I was supposed to. I question whether I was meant for this world, which I often - actually most days - find far too overwhelming and stressful. You know the film, *Final Destination*? Where they cheat death and then spend the rest of their lives running from it because they were supposed to die, and it won't stop until it's got them? Yep, I've often wondered whether I'm the real-life version of that. My life sometimes feels like one big chase and no matter where I hide, the shadows of death are always just around the corner.

I remember my childhood with confusion, mostly. My mum suffered from undiagnosed OCD, and my dad made her mental health problems undoubtedly a million times worse. He had a good way of getting inside people's heads and slowly, gently, almost without them realising it, tearing them down. He was very controlling, and yet came across as very charming to people on the outside. Little did they know that he was the king of affairs and spent some of his spare time indecently exposing himself to underage girls.

I've been told that at some point, there was somebody allocated to come and speak to my mum and dad together about why my dad did what he did and attempt to find ways to stop him from acting on his dark thoughts. Unbelievably, one tactic they suggested was to carry a photo of me. I often wonder how this situation would have panned out now, in the current day and age where these sorts of behaviours are taken seriously. I certainly doubt that looking at my innocent photo would be suggested as a distraction technique for an indecent exposer.

Obviously, I knew nothing of this and ignorance is bliss, as they say, so I adored my dad. He was my hero and I idolised him. Well, not so much when I was hiding behind the bedroom door with my brother, terrified of the screaming, shouting and smashing of plates and cupboard doors. Nor in a vivid memory of him putting his fist through the glass in the front door and seeing all the blood. But even then, I was more concerned for his wellbeing. Despite everything, I loved him very much and I still remember very clearly the day that he left and I heard the car driving away.

After dad left, my mum's OCD behaviours multiplied, and most of her time was spent cleaning obsessively. We couldn't have our breakfast until she'd finished her morning cleaning regime, and we weren't talking a quick flick-around with the duster. The place was, and still is, like a show home. Totally immaculate. The kind of place most people wish they could have.

I watched her in total frustration, rip down curtains off the poles after she'd spent however long analysing the width of the pleats and trying to make them all the same distance apart, and crying because she couldn't complete such an impossible task. I cried as my brother and I had to stand at opposite ends of the hall for what felt like an eternity for my little legs, because a small bit of paint had been chipped off the bathroom window and she went ballistic. I just remember standing there thinking, 'but I can't even reach that to have done it'.

Christmases were a mixed blessing. It was a time when a lot of alcohol-induced emotion was flying around by my mum, and I always felt very uncomfortable. But I do remember feeling very lucky when it came to presents. I got what seemed like an immense amount of toys and gifts; I had Barbies coming out of my ears - toys galore. Playing with them, however, was a separate issue.

My bedroom was like the rest of the house – immaculate, almost untouched, and that went for my toys too. They were pristine. I know now that I was forming the same thought processes and habits that I observed in my mum, and I needed everything to be perfect.

Toys had to be taken out for me and they were put away for me in their specific places. I always remember the big red bin of toys and all the toys behind it that I didn't dare pull out. One day, I dared to go over to my basket of rubber collections (I had a thing for rubbers and bouncy balls), balanced very precisely on my bookshelf, and look at them... then the basket fell... and so did my heart... right to the bottom of my feet... I frantically tried to put it all back together, but before I could, I was found out and told off. Back they were, put in their pristine, not-to-be-messed-with place.

I went to two of my friends' houses after school very frequently. I loved being there and I always found it strange to see what they ate for dinner, how their houses functioned and operated in chaos and mess, and how we could play freely. Friends never came to ours. Honestly, I don't think I really wanted them to. I was too scared that they would touch something or, God forbid, break something.

One friend came once. They wanted to play, to stand on my bed to see the shelf full of kinder egg toys that were spaced to perfection and – horror of horrors – they wanted to touch them! They created a domino effect and soon, my bed was creased, my teddies were moved, and now they were off to see something else, things that I didn't dare go near... and it was just horrendous. I just needed them to leave so everything could go back to where and how it should've been and be left alone - so that I could be left alone. I can't remember another friend visit after that.

I was late most days for school, even though it was a short walk. I think my mum liked to know her jobs were done before we left, and by the time I had navigated the anxiety of my socks being perfectly straight and rolled down so the folds were identical, time had always gotten away from us.

Years of dealing with my dad's indecent exposure habit, affairs and terrible treatment, a toxic mix of vile tempers and explosive rows, had torn my mum to the ground. The stress and anxiety of living with my dad plus her own demons made her life unbearable. She was depressed. But when he left, for some reason – probably because of how he'd made her feel adding to her own insecurities – she didn't think she could live without him, and she took numerous overdoses. I remember just the one.

I believe I was around seven, although the details escape me so I could have been younger, and there was a party going on next door. I couldn't find her. I looked around, but she wasn't there. I looked back at our house and the door was open, so I went in and saw her through the crack of the bathroom door. She looked like she was doing something strange in the bathroom mirror... in fact, she looked strange... not like herself. I opened the door and she was holding her tongue down, or trying to, but it all looked a bit strange and I knew something wasn't right. She was crying and trying to tell me to go back next door.

I went back next door and vaguely remember telling our neighbour that something wasn't right. I remember saying I wanted my dad, and being told that wasn't a good idea, and the next thing I know – or remember – is that my nan was there, I'm going to her house, and I'm none the wiser as to what has actually gone on.

My nan isn't technically my nan; she's my paternal grandfather's brother's wife - so like a great aunt by marriage. But I think of her, and it's easier to refer to her as, my nan. Whatever her actual family tie is, it doesn't really matter. What she actually is, is the shining light of my childhood and the reason I have memories of happy times. She gave me memories of things normal children remember. Creative activities (because playdough, paint and anything of the like were actually allowed at her house), days out, the park, learning to ride my bike, reading stories, playing shops, having a hamster, driving around seeing the Christmas lights, making Tracy Island from *Blue Peter* (or attempting to; those of my age will remember the pain). All of these things are my memories from being with my nan, and these memories are the saving grace of my childhood.

It got to the point where I was at my nan's more than I was at home. And although looking back, my best memories were made there, at the time I felt put out. My brother stayed at home with our mum, yet I was always at my nan's (or so it felt at the time), and I didn't understand why.

My nan was the one who took me to see mum at the hospital after her overdose. I remember holding the flowers and seeing thick gooey liquid next to her in a glass – which I'm now assuming was charcoal – but that's all I remember. I think I probably blanked most of it out, which I'm seemingly very talented at.

My dad picked me up on weekends from my nan's house. He was late quite a lot, or just didn't show up. I don't wish to think about what he may have been doing that was more important. When he did come, we went to various locations. Usually his sister's.

I was still only in junior school at this point, and right from nursery, I had struggled with it. In fact, I attempted playgroup before nursery, and I actually remember crying and thinking there was no way I was staying at that place. My nan says they used to take me through one door and I'd go out the other – there was not a chance they were going to get me in there, so the beginning and end of that merged into one fairly quickly!

After playgroup came nursery, and I didn't want to be there either. I was painfully shy and remember standing in the playground feeling like I wanted the ground to swallow me up. I kind of feel amazed looking back at that now, having my own daughter, that a child that young could feel such a way, but I did and I hated it. I was always by myself.

At school, I did make some close friends, and strangely enough, I could be a right bossy little madam! But anywhere else, I was painfully shy. All of my school reports said, 'Katie must ask for help when she needs it'. I hated putting my hand up, I hated being asked a question and I generally loathed anything that would bring attention to myself. My nan still laughs to this day about the fact that if we were ever out and about and someone said hello to me, I would not utter a single word but just fling a devastating death stare their way. I also would not go to school on my birthday; I point blank refused because the school did this torturous thing of getting the birthday boys and girls to the front of assembly to sing happy birthday and give them a sticker! This was the stuff nightmares were made of for me and there was no way I was going to be doing anything of the sort! If just one person sang happy birthday to me, I cried - let alone a whole school hall! No, thank you very much.

Most of my time at my nan's was spent creating, making (nothing changes to this day), reading, writing poetry and making myself a den between the back of the sofa and the radiator with a blanket over the top and one as a 'door' – that was my favourite place in the whole world, and I would spend hours in there, drawing and writing.

My dad got back together with someone he was with before he met my mum, and I spent more and more time with her two daughters and my new half-brother. I loved being there – it was the model of a perfect family: two girls who I could play with, a baby brother, a dog and a house I could be free in. I always felt sad going home to my mum and often cried. In my young mind, this was the perfect home and I absolutely adored my dad.

Slowly, little by little, I was there more and more. The weekends ran over longer than they should have, and talks started about me living there. I was around nine or ten, and all I saw in my mind was this perfect home, somewhere I loved being. My mum obviously sensed what was coming as she asked me one time when I went back, "You're going to live there aren't you?" I felt terrible.

Somewhere around this time, my mum was asked to go in to my school. She was being questioned about my welfare and accused of having multiple men over all the time. Basically, it was all worded to imply that she was not a capable parent. While some may have seen it that way, and even myself, now that I have a child, I disagree with much of how she was, I do not agree with it and still find it difficult to live with. My dad however, undoubtedly exaggerated some truths, and also, no doubt – filled some gaps with lies. A lot of what she did I found terribly hard to cope with and it still upsets me today – but I still loved her. She was my mum, the only mum I had.

My dad is good at talking, and a very convincing man. Apparently, the matter went to court somewhere in all of this. I was unaware, so I can't really comment. The fact of the matter is that somewhere along the line, I said I wanted to live with my dad. Looking back, is this memory 100% accurate? I'm not so sure, but the crux of the matter is that one weekend I went to my dad's and I never went home.

I remember being in the bath and hearing my dad on the phone to mum. I remember feeling sick and my heart pounding, but trying to act like it didn't matter. I remember them asking me if I wanted to speak to mum and me saying no… I didn't. I was so confused. It was all so quick; I didn't want a guilt trip from her and I couldn't bear to hear her cry, and so that was that. I didn't speak to her. In fact, I didn't speak to her for four years. As I said earlier, I have something of a talent for blocking things out, pretending they didn't happen and batting things from my mind like it happened to someone else in another life, on another planet.

The following years were somewhat of a blur. One second, I lived with my mum going to a school where I had a few close friends, and the next second, contact with my mum ceased – seemingly my own decision, but I had one very confused, young mind. I lived in a new house with a new family and was starting at a new school in the middle of a school year when friendship groups had already been made and sealed.

If I thought I struggled at school before, then this was just torture. I had no friends. For a while, my step sister was okay with me tagging along, but being the year above, she soon got fed up with this and told me I needed to find my own friends. Groups were already formed, and no one had time for the new girl who'd appeared mid-year, so I spent as many break times as I could in the toilets, on my own, just waiting for break to be over.

Eventually, the small group of unpopular kids took pity on me and offered their friendship, so I went along with it all and pretended that I'd found somewhere to fit in. The truth of the matter was, I didn't feel like I fit in anywhere. I'd go to bed and cry to myself that I wanted my mum and that I wanted to go home – a secret that I couldn't possibly tell anyone after all the hassle and all the fall out. After all, ten years old or not, this was my decision, right?! This was what I had chosen and so I needed to deal with it.

When I was fourteen, I remember being in Greece on holiday, and me and my step mum were going for a walk where we spoke about me making contact with my mum. I remember being reluctant to do this to begin with, although I don't remember exactly why. I think in a lot of ways, I had bad memories and was just extremely confused by how I felt in general.

I did make contact with my mum after that, though. I wrote her a letter (in the terrible times of no mobile phones) and added a photo, telling her about me being a keen runner and into athletics, the multiple five-star athletics awards I'd had from school, and whatever else that I had deemed important at the time.

Eventually, we met up. It felt right but wrong all at the same time. Right, because deep down I'd obviously missed her for 4 years – she's my mum, of course I did – but there were so many conflicting feelings of guilt and confusion. It was almost like I was looking at my life from the outside sometimes, like I was just going along with what I thought or hoped might be best, to somehow make everyone else feel better, even though I spent most of my time feeling guilty about pretty much everything. Some things clearly never change. Can you believe I still have the Mr. Man tissue that I soaked with my tears during that reunion with my mum? I keep it in a box of random things that have bewildering sentiments attached to them.

I moved to senior school and made a small group of close friends. We were kind of the floaties in the middle, neither the popular girls nor the 'geeks' but just a small group, floating somewhere in between. They were all great girls and I loved our little group. One remains my best friend to this day.

I floated through, and kept to myself where possible. I got picked on at one point for the shape of my head, which maybe has a larger circumference than others – I think due to me being premature – and I never wore my hair up because of this. However, if anyone picked on me, it never lasted long as they'd often be taken aback with my own sharp venom, or in a couple of cases, a punch that they weren't expecting. I definitely wasn't one for taking crap from anyone – I certainly wouldn't take it lying down.

The same went for home. As I got older, my temper flared. There were frequent rows with both step sisters, one in particular who felt my rage and quite often my fist. In one red mist rage, I chased her with a knife and recall feeling my step mum pull me off her as I had her around the throat up against the wall.

Me and my step mum were like cats and dogs. We didn't get on and it was a toxic household for me. Gone were the days where I loved being a part of this 'perfect' family. I felt I didn't fit in, like I was on the outside looking in all the time at a family I didn't belong with. That's how I felt, day in and day out, it was like a ball that constantly sat heavy in my stomach every day.

I never was sure what to call my step mum – it was another elephant in the room. On the one hand, I didn't want to call her by her name as that made me feel like an outsider when she was 'mum' to the other three. Part of me wanted to be able to call her mum too. The other part of me knew that I had a mum of my own. So, I would just avoid calling her anything. When I wanted her attention, I just made sure I was in direct view and hoped my hesitancy to refer to her verbally would go unnoticed. It did for a while. Inevitably, however, the cringeworthy topic was raised and my insides crawled with awkwardness and embarrassment.

Then others would tell me that it was upsetting her. I can understand as an adult that this would be frustrating, a little bewildering and probably upsetting. But the daily impact that this was having on me went completely unnoticed. It may have been a small thing to others, but it was a huge deal to me.

One day, my step mum announced that unless I called her something when I spoke to her, she would not answer. I can still remember how that felt. It may have seemed like I was being ignorant or rude, but what was behind the nameless conversations ran a lot deeper. I started to call her by her name, cringing each time as the others called her mum. On birthdays and special occasions, I alternated between sending her cards with 'mum' on the front, and others addressing her by her name. The 'mum' cards made her happy and I liked the way we got on in those moments. Although, if I'm honest, neither ever felt right to me. I felt odd no matter what I did. This frustrated me; I just wanted to feel like I fit in somewhere. When me and my step mum got on well, I glowed inside. It made me so happy. But inevitably, especially as I got older, it was mostly rowing and bickering.

No one saw the marks from my cutting. I had a long-sleeved shirt and blazer for school, and I made sure no one saw a thing. It was my secret. My thing. Something that no one knew. Something I had tucked away as a handy back-up for when things got too much. It was mine.

THE RAZOR OF REASON

The self-harm continued. Most of the time, it was just superficial and always with a razor blade. It felt like a release, and it helped to calm me down when I could have easily hurt someone else or put my head through a window. Instead, I contained it to an area, and in a way that no one could see.

When I was 16, I felt like I was living in hell. The tense relationships at home, mixed with general anger and a large helping of teenage hormones, made me angrier, more frustrated and more depressed.

There was a lad who'd started working in the shop over the road and I liked him. He was older than me – I think he was 21 at the time – and I liked him more for that. Boys my own age didn't interest me, and I certainly didn't fancy anyone at school. I got to talking to him one day and we ended up going out. My dad gave him the 'if you hurt her, I will kill you' speech. He wasn't happy about him being older, which was ironic, given that he saw younger girls himself..

I revised like a demon for my GCSEs and came away with 10 A-C grades. I decided that I wanted to go to a performing arts college. While I was quiet and liked to keep to myself, I had been in drama class for a few years (paid for by my trusty paper round), and I was really dedicated to it. I used to print out monologues and practice them in my room.

My dad was not happy about it, he wanted me to do A-levels. I think the only time anyone expressed any interest in my desire to act was when I got an audition for the TV-drama, *Doctors.* I was 15 or so, and all of a sudden there was some excitement around it. I was allowed a day off school to go to the audition (where I ended up getting smacked in the face by a woman because it was in the script – I bet they don't allow that anymore!) Of course, it was Nan and my best friend who accompanied me in the taxi, not my dad. After the audition, I never heard anything from them and I felt like an absolute failure.

But I wasn't going to be deterred from college. I applied and got an audition. I spent ages looking over the different monologues I could do. Something filled with rage probably would have suited me well at that time, but while sitting in my English GCSE class one day, I found myself staring at Tom Leonard's poem 'Six O'clock News'.

this is thi
six a clock
news thi
man said n
thi reason
a talk wia
BBC accent
iz coz yi
widny wahnt
mi ti talk
aboot thi
trooth wia
voice lik
wanna yoo
scruff. if
a toktaboot
thi trooth
lik wanna yoo
scruff yi
widny thingk
it wuz troo.
jist wanna yoo
scruff tokn.
thirza right
way ti spell
ana right way
to tok it. this
is me tokn yir
right way a
spellin. this
is ma trooth.
yooz doant no
thi trooth
yirsellz cawz

yi canny talk
right. this is
the six a clock
nyooz. belt up.

The choice of poem has its ironies given my life at the time. But I was drawn to it. And when I realised I could do an alright Scottish accent – that was it, that was my audition piece.

The audition went well. I had tutors come up to me afterwards to say it was great and some students acted surprised when I spoke without a Scottish accent. I came away feeling proud and shortly after, I received my acceptance letter.

The school prom came and went in a blur. There was one person from school who I liked; we often walked home from school together and he asked me to the prom, but then he spent the majority of the evening with my friend (who also liked him).

I wore a long, red, glittery dress from Miss Selfridge. I went to choose the dress myself and used my paper round money to pay for it. I was jealous of my step sister who, the year before, had been bought a 'proper dress', and of my best friend who also had a 'proper dress', but I felt good in it all the same. Although, I do remember feeling upset that night because my dad and step mum were out, so there was no one to see me off or take photos of me arriving – I remember seeing the other parents waiting for their children's limos to arrive to take photos. Our limo was late to the prom because we just drove around for a while drinking. I turned up quite tipsy and I don't remember too much from the night.

IN BLOOM NOT BROKEN

At this point, I had stopped self-harming and things felt better. School was over, which I was happy about; I was in a relationship and spent most of my waking hours at his house, so I wasn't on my own as much feeling like I wanted to smash things; and I had been accepted, with praise, into a college that I really wanted to go to. Things were better, even if my dad barely spoke to me.

I had to get on an early bus to college every morning. There was usually a lot of noise and weed smoking on the top deck, which was a bit of a shock first thing in the morning. I've never been a morning person and people close to me generally know to leave me alone until I've had a morning cup of tea and a cigarette.

My best friend had decided to go to the same college to do the same course. She has since said, bless her heart, that she really only went because I was going and she didn't really know what she wanted to do.

I'd been imagining how good it would be to act all day with my best friend by my side, but fairly quickly, this dream was destroyed. There were actually very few drama classes; we had to go to dancing and singing lessons too, which I wasn't good at.

People formed friendships quickly, and it was almost like I wasn't part of the course. They sat together at lunch on large tables. My best friend had become friends with a group of A-level girls, and so I spent my lunches feeling like I did when I moved schools after leaving my mum, wandering the halls or hiding in the toilets.

Me and my best friend have since spoken about this and we actually had a good laugh, because she felt like she didn't fit in with the arts crowd, and thought that I had! She wasn't as happy with her new group as I had believed. Somehow, we had managed to create an invisible barrier between us, when actually we were feeling pretty similar. Ah, that's good old teenage angst for you right there.

My mood went downhill, and the razor and long sleeves came back out. I had to fight to do the course, sticking to my guns that this is what I wanted, how could I possibly tell anyone that it wasn't working out?

So, I carried on getting up early, being stressed all day and arriving home absolutely exhausted. Somewhere along the way, I managed to make a friend and then I made friends with her friends, and I was so incredibly grateful that these people wanted to spend time with me. Although, once again I felt like an outsider looking in, like someone who'd just gate-crashed a friendship group. I was just grateful to not be on my own.

My boyfriend, who I was still spending most of my time with, found out about the self-harming. He already knew about the depression – that was getting worse by the day and resulted in many rows and floods of tears from me. I had lost my virginity to him, so I suppose it was inevitable that he would find out.

He convinced me to go to the doctor, and here began my first of many diabolical dealings with the National Health Service regarding mental health. I tried to explain to the doctor how I was feeling, but they just looked confused... flicking through a book, asking me questions like if I was being bullied at school. Finally, they said that they 'really didn't know what was wrong' and I was given a prescription for antidepressants. I never told anyone about them and took them in secret, but they made me feel sick and spaced out.

IN BLOOM NOT BROKEN

I was on the phone to my mum one day and I got upset. I can't remember exactly what I said, but I told her that I had been given antidepressants and that no one knew. She told my dad and step mum. There was a row. I was taken off the pills and that was the end of that.

One day, I was called into the garden by my dad and step mum and they told me that they knew I was self-harming. I cannot explain the feeling of utter dread that came over me. I cannot remember exactly what I said, although I know that I did a lot of shouting. They asked me why I would do such a thing and if I wanted to kill myself, they even told me that I was cutting the wrong way if I wanted to die. I remember that my step mum did most of the talking. I don't remember what my dad thought about it all and I don't ever remember having a proper chat with him about how I was feeling or what was going on in my head.

I still get mad inside when I think about that day in the garden, especially now that I have a child – God, if I ever found out she was self-harming, I would hold her and tell her to talk to me and that I would never judge her for it and that I needed to know what was going on in her life. But for me, it was just another thing that was shouted about and then brushed under the carpet, like something invisible to the naked eye but it still hurts every time someone treads on the damn thing.

I spent so much of my time crying and just being so utterly and deeply miserable. I hated being at home. My step mum and I rowed all the time and I hardly spoke to my dad – this man who I had adored became a person that I avoided. And so, I stayed at my boyfriend's house as much as possible. We split up a couple of times over the few years I was with him and we rowed a lot. We were both young, in each other's pockets all the time, and I was self-harming more and more. My mood followed me around like a big black shadow. I felt desperately alone with it all.

One day, it all came out that I was deeply unhappy about college. I said I didn't want to go anymore and I got the, 'I'm not going to say I told you so' speech (in other words, the 'I told you so' speech). I went to college and booked an appointment with a career advisor. When it was time for my appointment, my class tutor said in front of the whole class, "Katie's got to go for her careers appointment now as she's decided she's too good for us all." Haha, the irony! If only he'd known that the truth was the complete opposite.

After that day, I never went back. I had failed at my dream. The razor was my comfort and the cuts zigzagged my legs, since I'd realised legs were easier to cover up.

One day, I returned home from a night at my boyfriend's. Nothing unusual about that... but when I arrived, I was informed that the police had been there going through all our stuff, even our underwear drawers. It was something to do with dad and child pornography.

The ins and outs of what happened escape me. But it was something to do with a hard drive and my dad's work at his garage. Dad had tried to blame another family member who worked with him. He was innocent, but because of my dad's narcissistic behaviour, he nearly had his kids taken away from him. I really don't remember much and I don't even really remember reacting to it at the time. Most likely, I tried to shrug it off and pretend that nothing had happened - my dad wouldn't do this.

It's worth noting here that I didn't know about the child pornography or incidents of indecent exposure before that night. I was too young when it had happened and had lost contact with my mum during my teenage years, so it wasn't something she would have told me about. I wanted to pretend it wasn't true – and he will say until the cows come home that it's all a pack of lies – but I have spoken to more than one family member about it and I know the truth. It's a truth that hurts – especially when you know that you'll never hear it from the person you need to.

I left college and started looking for a job. In the days before internet, I actually hand wrote letters and made phone calls to nursery after nursery. Fairly quickly, I secured a job as a children's assistant in a local nursery (ironically I got my worst GCSE grade, a D, in child development, but that was primarily because it was a rowdy class and the tutor spent most of the time running out of the room in tears).

The job saved me, and I loved it… for a while.

That black fog caught up with me and the 'razor of reason' became my friend once again. The cuts got deeper and more frequent and I wasn't happy unless there was a sufficient amount of blood to satisfy my increasingly erratic brain. Soon it wasn't for the release, it was to hurt myself. I didn't do it to hurt anyone else or for any kind of attention. In fact I would have done anything for no one to know about it – a common assumption about self-harm is that self-harmers are attention seekers or they want to die. They aren't, and they don't; they just want to kill a small piece of themselves that hurts like hell, that hurts more than any razor or cut ever could.

I called in sick more and more, and then just stopped going – a trend that was to continue in pretty much every job I'd ever have.

I had started smoking weed and I loved it, loved the feeling, loved the fact that I was doing something else that no one knew about and that I had yet another little vice up my sleeve to dull the noise in my head.

However, one day I smoked too much and had a huge 'whitey' (as it is known). I have never felt so sick in my life. If you've ever had travel sickness or been on a waltzer ride where you feel like your world has lost all equilibrium and you can literally feel the colour draining from your face, multiply that by about 100 and that is what a 'whitey' feels like.

I often ended up crying at my nan's house because I'd had yet another shouting match with my step mum, who could be absolutely vile (although it wasn't all one way, I had a vicious tongue too and could be explosive). Sometimes I'd hear her telling my dad that I'd said things that I hadn't; my dad would rarely listen to my side of the story, which was unbearably frustrating. I used to write down things that she'd said to me and how I was feeling; maybe as proof and so I wouldn't forget that I was being made to feel like a liar an awful lot. Both my diaries from that time completely vanished, even though I'd hidden them from everyone else, they were never to be seen again. They were never spoken about, just pushed under the ever-bulging rug and ceased to exist. But the pain each time someone trod on the damn thing, it was becoming ever harder to ignore.

I'd often hit my sisters for whatever row or reason I saw fit. I felt like I didn't want to be anywhere. Definitely not inside my own skin. Most of the time I couldn't stand myself, and I didn't know what to do with myself. One day, drugs seemed to be the obvious choice. Not weed, I was done with that. Something more exciting.

COCAINE FRIDAYS

Most people would probably tell you that they first took drugs because they were offered them at a party, or they were peer-pressured in to it. Not me. In true 'me' style, it was a completely planned event; my choice of drug, my choice of when and where. Next for me on the narcotic table were pills, or ecstasy, as it's formally known.

My boyfriend and I had planned to go to a club called Sundissential: a dingy hard house venue that sometimes, quite literally, had sweat dripping from the ceiling. It sounds vile, but for someone into the hard house scene this was a much-loved venue, one of the best there was.

We found someone in the club selling, and down went half – I felt nothing. Zip. Nada. I mean how long would it take to work? Shouldn't it be doing something by now? Back to the toilets and down went the other half. And I wait.

All of a sudden, I can't move. Who the hell turned the music up? Did the lights just get brighter? And why do I feel like I can't open my jaw? I'm stuck. I'm literally stuck on this chair. My legs don't work. They actually don't work.

I turn to my boyfriend and say, "I'm stuck, I'm actually glued to the chair." He gets me up and we dance a little. Now I feel so light. Like if I jumped, my feet would just float up and up and I'd never come back down. Wouldn't that be nice? I could just live in the clouds. I could so do that. So, I jump. But I come back down. Now I feel sick and I'm shivering from head to toe. And it's so loud. I want to go home.

When we get home, I look in the mirror and my eyes are huge and my pupils are black. I declare that I am never, ever, *ever*, doing that again.

So the next week, I do it again. And the following week, and pretty regularly after that. Mostly I would do it at my boyfriend's house, in his room or walking around outside. It felt absolutely amazing! We talked and talked about stuff that seemed so important at the time. But more importantly, it completely numbed any sense of myself and my feelings. I just felt light and incredible… after puking a few times in various bushes.

I loved those weekends so much. And I wanted more. Something else. Something I'd been offered a few times but had always said no to because it had to be on my terms. Well I'd thought about it, and I'd decided that I wanted to try coke. Not the fizzy drink kind - cocaine.

I was more nervous the first time I tried cocaine than I had been when I tried pills. It had more of an addict's reputation, a harder drug. I was half expecting to do it and be out for the count, like someone who had just done heroin.

Compared to the pills, I was surprised at the speed at which it worked, and the buzz. It was amazing. I loved it. I felt fearless. My confidence skyrocketed after a few lines and I felt utterly invincible. And so I had found my new weekend best friend.

My boyfriend and I were arguing more and more, having rows in the street. And with the inevitable comedowns, my mood was getting more unpredictable. He would sometimes get a little strange from the drugs. It was irresponsible of us because he was taking other medications too, and I don't know if that's why, but I do know that the drink-and-drug combo was definitely not for him. One night, I awoke to his hands in places where they shouldn't have been; he was climbing on top of me and telling me that 'I know you want to.' I pushed him off and luckily, under the influence of substances, that was the end of that.

I started spending more time with one of his friends. We'd always absolutely hated each another, for no real reason. If he came in, I would leave the room and vice versa. If we passed each other, we would mutter comments about the other being a dickhead (or something equally as charming). But somewhere along the line, we started talking – I believe it was over the borrowing of a hard house CD – and we become close. We started meeting up in secret and spending more and more time together. Before we knew it, we were going off together for weekends in hotels, getting utterly smashed on coke.

Of course, it eventually came out, but I didn't care. I had it bad for this bloke – also about four years older than me – and I loved spending time with him. They say that there's a fine line between love and hate, and in this case, it couldn't have been closer to the truth.

I got a new job, and here I found the person who would be my best friend for some years to come. We started talking and discovered that we went to the same clubs and that she used to 'do stuff', but not anymore. Well, with my powers of persuasion, she was soon out on that dance floor with me.

I didn't last long at that job either. I didn't like it. I went through another period of depression and would find myself crying before I even got to work; it took all the will in the world to get me through the door. One day I just left.

I started a new job. It was further away – funnily enough, in the same town as my old college – and it was in a big office full of people. I actually liked it, and discovered that I was good at upselling – good at convincing people they really needed a call back to change their gas and electric supplier. I was often the top seller and won prizes on a pretty regular basis. I met another girl there who joined our weekend gang and we had the time of our lives.

Now, I'm not advocating for drugs. I'm not saying that drugs are good. But I'm not going to lie; these were some of the best days of my life and I do not regret this period for one second. My life had been filled with so much chaos and problems that it felt so good to have a boyfriend whom I loved and a group of genuine friends that I could be myself around to go to clubs I loved, with music I loved. I was taking ecstasy and cocaine regularly, but it was at a recreational level. I wasn't doing it every day, it wasn't like I lived for it (although I did live for the weekends, so I guess that's debatable!).

I went to festivals in fluffy boots and face paints. I'd come back with mud up to my knees after 24 hours of solid partying. I went to clubs, took five pills a night and had amazing experiences speaking utter rubbish to random people, dancing until the sweat dripped off my chin and I was red in the face (I've got some horrendous photos from back then – ones where it looks like my eyes are pointing in the opposite directions). I went to random after-parties in the backs of vans, where people just piled in united by a night of drugs and freedom. I really had the best times with the best people.

Looking back, it wasn't the safest choices. And I should add that there were also less favourable parts; like taking too much and throwing up. Or trying ketamine at an after-party and going into a K hole – which is basically like passing out, like you don't exist, but you're probably doing something embarrassing or speaking absolute tosh to people around you whilst projectile vomiting in a random person's toilet.

At points in my life, I have dipped my toes into the waters of addiction but it's never been full blown. I've always managed to pull myself back. But it could have gone the other way. For the most part though, this was a time in my life that I had worked out my limits, taking just enough to have a good night. I carried on clubbing like this for a good few years.

I held down my job. I got headhunted by the sales department, and for my age I was earning a decent wage with good commission. My dad seemed almost proud of me when I'd go home and tell him about the commission I'd made. My step sister was at college doing the A-levels he so desperately wanted me to do, but he seemed genuinely pleased with me and that felt great.

I loved my boyfriend and we moved out and rented our own flat. This day was one of the best of my life. My own flat with someone I loved. I was elated. Free to do whatever I pleased, whenever I pleased. No more rowing, no more sharing rooms, just me and him and peace and quiet. The first night that we closed those doors, we cracked out the cocaine and it was bliss.

For a while, it was great. Soon though, the honeymoon phase came to an end and that black shadow hunted me down once again. Worse than ever before. It hunted me down and it got me by the throat. I started feeling extremely depressed; and this time, it wasn't lifting. Nothing helped. Nothing made it better.

We would go and visit my dad and step mum and for some reason, every time we left, I was hit with a huge wave of guilt. Had I stayed long enough? Did they think I was trying to get away? Did my dad know I loved him? Looking back, it was silly and I have no idea why it happened. But guilt had become one of my primary emotions. Guilt for everything and everyone; guilt just for being me, for being alive.

I named the road I walked along to go to work 'The Road of Doom.' It was an industrial estate and was grey and depressing. I would stop before the dreaded walk and just cry. Many times, I walked back to the train station, called in sick and went home.

I was still going out and having a good time; I used the weekends and the drugs, mostly coke, to block out what was going on in my head and to make it through the week. I convinced myself that I was exhausted from the journey to work, the getting up early and getting home late, and that getting a new job would make the problem disappear. So, I went for a new job closer by.

It was a small new office and everyone was starting together. I liked that. The commission wasn't as good, but it was mostly selling the same services and I knew what I was doing. When I was feeling better, I did well. I was naturally good at sales, but my perfectionist nature and the pressure I put on myself to constantly be the best was a toxic combination.

In a sales environment, the cocaine tends to fly around. Pretty much everyone in the office was doing it. Even the manager did it (she was either popping to powder her nose regularly or had a very weak bladder). Myself and a couple of female friends used to call it 'Coke Fridays' because I would come to work on a Friday with a little sealed plastic bag for each of us, with our name and a smiley face drawn on it. I remember standing there one Friday, looking around the office, and laughing to myself because pretty much everyone was buzzing from cocaine.

I had one bad experience. I was with my boyfriend in a hotel before we had moved out of home. We had been doing cocaine for two or three nights in a row and drinking, which isn't a good mix. It was the last line... actually, it could have been the last three lines. By this point I'd been doing it a while and I thought I was invincible. Up it went. Within seconds, I knew something wasn't right. Everything had slowed down, where it normally sped up. I felt heavy, the opposite of what I normally felt. Everything looked and sounded wrong. I stood up and everything moved. My heart was pounding. I felt sick and couldn't breathe.

It was clear that it wasn't good. I threw up and made myself throw up again, hoping it would clear my system. My boyfriend put me in the shower in the hope that it would do something, but it wasn't working. An ambulance was mentioned, but then so were the 'what ifs' about the police. I could barely talk and I thought I was going to die. This was it. This was my end; a cocaine overdose.

I stood there looking at my boyfriend speaking to me, but I couldn't hear him. Why was he walking backwards? Why was he getting smaller? He started echoing and I thought to myself, 'that's it, I'm about to die, I'm actually going to die - and my dad is going to kill him.' And everything went black.

I opened my eyes. I was on the floor and all I could hear was a high-pitched ringing in both my ears. My boyfriend's mouth was moving but I couldn't hear his words. The situation was not improving and so, after disposing of everything, he called an ambulance.

The paramedic was lovely, but the hospital staff weren't my biggest fans. After a few hours of checks and observation, I was let go. We went back to the hotel and threw away all the drugs and paraphernalia. We vowed to never touch that white powder again.

We spent the following night in another hotel so that I could recover. The next day, I remember going home, giving my dad a hug and saying goodnight. I thought how weird it was that he had no idea about any of it. And how I had thought I would never get to go home. I really thought I was going to die. For a while, I noticed things I wouldn't have previously noticed and was grateful for things that I wouldn't have thought twice about before. But inevitably, it passed. And so did the vow of a narcotic-free life. I carried on going out and having white weekends. Although I was a lot more cautious than before.

My black cloud continued to follow me around and I put on a pretence at work. My boyfriend spent most of his time with his mates and I sank lower and lower. I just carried on, with a painted mask on my face, day after day after day. But it was becoming difficult to keep up. I had a few bust ups with people at work, a couple that nearly escalated into fights. My moods were up down quicker than I could blink. I was either the life and soul of the party, or couldn't even bear to speak to anyone.

THE DEEPER YOU FALL

I have always loved my holidays and I was looking forward to a Spain getaway to escape. But unfortunately, I had to take myself with me.

I remember so clearly being at the hotel buffet, standing in front of the Spaghetti Bolognese. I was starving after a hot day and it smelled and looked so good. But this inner rage built inside me as I looked at it. I wanted to eat it... but I was fat... so I couldn't ...but I wanted to ... but I'd get more fat... but I was hungry... but you'll eat it and instantly swell to the size of a house, look at your stomach, look at your arms... and you're going to eat that?

The inner dialogue and frustration was unreal. I felt like there was a Mike Tyson boxing match going on in my stomach. And all the while, I could smell the food. I got so agitated that I cried. I couldn't explain why to anyone, I just fled the room.

The torture in that moment was indescribable. I couldn't make sense of all the thoughts. All I knew was that I was utterly disgusting. And feeding that disgusting feeling was only going to make it grow and fester. But I discovered that I could feed that feeling... and throw it up.

I remember going around the supermarket after we arrived home and deciding that I would only eat Weight Watcher meals. I would study the calorie content on the backs of every packet and pick the readymade meals with the lowest calorie count.

At work, I was in and out of the toilets punching my stomach and pinching the rolls of fat harder and harder, wishing I could rip them off. I started eating less and less and struggled more and more to get myself to work.

The depression had hit. There was no mood fluctuation, no great mood spikes amongst the black. Just very dark black all the time.

I started a diary at the beginning of what was to become to a fully-fledged eating disorder. One of the first things in it is a poem:

The blackness of oblivion – it seems to know my name

Sometimes it whispers, sometimes it screams,

But it's there all the same,

For so long I've shaken from its grip

But I feel that I'm beginning to slip

All I want is blackness, darkness, nothing more

Colours and things they hurt my eyes

I can't work out what they're for,

Life hurts so much – it's painful just 'being'

I just can't see what they're all seeing

I don't want to be living, I don't want to be me,

But people don't understand or see,

'It'll get better', 'it'll be fine' they say

But if they were me for just one day

Then maybe they'd realise I'm better off dead

It'd be so much better than living in my head,

If an animal is in pain, they put it down,

Well I'm in pain so why does everyone frown?

When I say I want to be out of pain too,

Why am I always told that I will pull through?

I don't want to hurt people, only me,

I don't shove it in people's faces for them all to see

People try to help but I just feel so low

I wish they could accept it and let me go

It hurts to smile, it hurts to live a lie

When all I want to do is close my eyes and die.

***

One day, a row with my manager about the commission structure was the straw that broke the camel's back in my plummeting mood and weight obsession. I was making myself sick after meals. In fact, not just meals; pretty much after I ate anything at all.

At work, I was training people on sales and there was talk of me having a supervisor role. But for some reason, it never happened. I was frustrated and I'd had enough. One day, I walked out on my lunch break, walked down the road and before I knew it, I was on the bus home. My phone was ringing and people were leaving me messages saying that if I came back, we would talk about a promotion. But I just turned my phone off and carried on home. I walked through my front door, shut it and breathed a huge sigh of relief.

My diary entries from this time refer to my ex-boyfriend a lot and for the purpose of this book, I will call him Rob. I do not wish to trigger anyone with any numbers and weights referred to in these diary excerpts, though I have done my best to remove the majority. But I do feel that it's necessary to show that there is no 'happy number' in anorexia; there is never a weight that someone with an eating disorder will be happy with, that will make them stop. It simply doesn't exist. The deeper you go, the deeper you fall, and the harder it is to get out. I also wish to highlight that someone can have all the anorexic thoughts and feelings, but not yet be at an 'anorexic weight.'

Monday 9th October 2006

I don't really know why I bought this to write stuff in. I just feel crap like, what's the point? No one really knows how I feel. I wish I could just tell my dad and he could give me a hug – but I can't.

To make things worse, I weighed myself and I'm like more than what I thought I was, and I weighed myself on two separate sets of scales in boots. I feel really angry about that. In a way, I'm thinking, 'what's the fucking point?' After all I'm still at my regular weight and I just feel like eating. On the other hand, I think that I've got to carry this on – the second being more prominent, I guess.

It's like a battle in my head: 'Eat, don't eat, be sick' ALL. THE. TIME. I'm hungry and I want to eat, but how I feel afterwards really isn't worth it. It's all so confusing. It really is because I THINK this isn't all about the weight, but then the way I feel about putting weight on and the way I feel today after weighing myself, surely it must be?

Rob has just gone on nights and I have done what I have thought about all day; I've just spent half an hour in the bathroom making myself sick. I still feel so dodgy and it's nearly six hours later! I really thought I might pass out.

Why do I do this? This is what I feel like every time I do it and I always swear that I won't do it again tomorrow, but I always do. And I know I'll wake up tomorrow and do it all over again.

It's not nice not trusting your own thoughts.

The fucked-up thing is even though I feel shit health-wise, in my head I feel so much calmer after I've been sick – like I've done what I was supposed to do.

Although I have constant thoughts about food and all this, the one thing that is making me feel less anxious and less stressed/angry at the moment is being out of work. It feels like a huge weight has been lifted off my shoulders, but how do I tell Rob? How do I tell him that I'm not ready to go back to work without sounding like an idiot and like I'm completely taking the piss?

Every day I wake up, I feel empty (if it wasn't for Rob at the moment, I think things could be a lot worse), and not having to deal with people and work just helps.

I've made so many excuses lately for people not to come around, I just feel like I can't deal with talking about silly things, stuff that doesn't even matter. So just being at home at the moment is good, but I just don't know how to tell Rob.

God, I feel like an idiot – I'm sitting here feeling sick and shaky, yet I can't eat and I'm here writing all of this when no one is ever even going to read it!

Rob is such an angel – he doesn't understand all of this and how much is really going on, but I do love him so much.

The beginning of an eating disorder is such a confusing place. The thoughts don't make sense, the feelings are conflicting, and the inner turmoil is unbearable.

Contrary to popular belief, anorexics do not *not* like food! Pretty much every person in the throes of anorexia, including myself, will tell you that's bullshit. Food doesn't suddenly become repellent. Actually, the opposite happens. The hungrier someone with an eating disorder becomes, the more they will study food: look at it, smell it, touch it, chew it and spit it back out. Feeding makes us feel sick with guilt, but the desire for the food and the taste intensifies. We're just so damn terrified of those numbers going up on that torture device called 'the scale', and how it is going to make us feel.

My diary from this period contains another poem:

Where does she go?

How does she get out of this?

Where does she go?

Who does she tell of all her sorrow?

The tears that cloud up her eyes

Filled with sadness as she cries

A vicious cycle hard to break

All of this so hard to take

A constant battle in her mind

All the willpower she's trying to find

To say no to the thoughts that fill her head

Instead listen to the things that are being said

But it's just no good – thoughts always win

Get louder and louder until it becomes a din

So does she eat and purge or not eat at all?

Either way she's set to fall

But these seem to be the only choices

With her mind so filled with all these voices

It becomes not a choice

But more a must

And which of these does she trust?

It makes no difference – there's no way through

She just wished that she could tell all of you.

I decided that I needed to train in something and so I started a nail technician course. I liked the idea of the creativity in nail art. I was good at painting tiny detail onto tiny nails, and the tutor was impressed with my ability.

My obsession with food, weight and keeping down all the things I ate was becoming a daily preoccupation.

Tuesday 10th October 2006

I feel so shit today! My chest is tight, I feel dizzy, and of course when Rob asks if I'm ok I say, 'I'm fine' when all I actually want to do is cry. How long can I carry this on for?

When Rob asks me if I want to eat, it's like my body takes on its own voice that isn't necessarily my own and I end up shaking and just saying no.

Those numbers are still on the table to phone for job applications, but I literally can't bring myself to ring them.

I watched this YouTube video earlier of a girl who was 26, although now recovered, she started all this when she was 20. She said that she was 'fine' for a year like, 'Hey you hear all this stuff, but I'm fine!'

Then she said it started with her hair falling out (which has started happening to me) and she was like, 'No big deal, it's still worth it, right?' Same as me... but then her toenails fell off... she got a weak bladder, weak bones, and lots of really awful stuff. Even now, even though she's recovered, she has just had to have a load of teeth taken out and she has to have iron injections, has a weak heart, etc.

It hit home. But is it really enough to stop all of this? I'm not so sure, I still have this voice in my head going, 'Well you're not and will not get that bad, so you don't need to worry.' Is this true?

I've told myself I will not make myself sick tomorrow, I'm determined to try and stop this path.

I have my appointment with the counsellor on Monday. ME... a counsellor! It all seems so ridiculous.

Anorexia is a sneaky illness. It creeps up on you slowly, it makes you sly, it makes your mind work in quite mysterious ways and it makes you a plotting genius.

Friday 20th October 2006

Well Rob is on about telling my dad – doesn't he realise that this will just make things worse but not actually achieve anything as I'd just eat more around people and throw it up later. There are ways and means...

I feel worthless today and Rob has just confirmed it; apparently, I look like 'a bag of shit.'

He's said that all this is affecting our relationship. I'm fucking everything up and I don't deserve him.

He said, 'When I say no to food, I'm saying yes to all the bad things and dying.' Well good. At the moment, I don't deserve anything else. I don't want to let Rob down or my dad - specifically my dad - I NEED for him not to know.

Looking back, it was such a huge deal to me that my dad didn't find out about my anorexia. It caused me a tremendous amount of anxiety and stress. I couldn't bear to see that look in his eyes that told me I was a disappointment. I desperately wanted approval, and this most certainly wasn't the way to get it.

Tuesday 24th October 2006

I saw Sue, the counsellor, yesterday and we talked about a lot of things that I don't usually talk about. She said that it sounds like I find it hard to ask for help and never tell people of bad things, or don't like to because of the way I've been brought up. I don't like to disappoint people and I don't like to bring attention to issues. I hate all this, I don't even know what to do anymore.

Thursday 2nd November 2006

I feel like I'm losing myself – that I'm just 'here' and I don't feel anything. My life is just food, that's the only thing that I can control and feel. That doesn't really even make any sense does it? Oh well.

I feel so down, all I can think about is not being here anymore. I feel like cutting or purging, because the razor has become my friend again but to be honest, at the moment, I can't even be bothered to do that! All I want is to go somewhere where no one can find me, curl up in a ball and die.

If it wasn't for Rob, my Dad, my nan and my mum, and the upset I'd cause, I swear to God I would. They are literally the only things stopping me right now.

I'm actually sitting here on the bed with a load of paracetamol by my side – I don't even know why, it's not like I'm going to do it... I don't think... it's like a comfort blanket, I guess. I just want to cease to exist.

Sunday 5th November 2006

All Rob does at the moment is go out, which I can't blame him for. I'd no doubt want to go out and leave me too – I want to leave myself for God's sake, so I can't blame someone else for wanting to but I wrote him a letter last night telling him exactly how I've been feeling; that I'd been thinking about dying and just not being here anymore. I gave it him before he went out at 6:30 pm, he texted me once all night and came back at 1:30 am throwing up.

I know it's not all about me, but it took such a lot to write that letter and it just seemed like he didn't give a flying fuck! I slept in the spare room and finally fell asleep at 4:00 am and when I get up, he's not fucking here again!

Friday 10th November 2006

I haven't written in here as often – my head is really screwed up and I just forget, I keep forgetting a lot of things lately.

I went to see Sue again yesterday, and we talked mainly about my eating and health. I told her pretty much everything, and she looked quite concerned at points and like she didn't really know what to do, but I like her and I trust her which doesn't happen very often.

She said she's going to write me a letter to take to the doctors which is so, so scary, but I guess I will have to go. She said with the way I'm going, I will end up being sectioned and have to get treatment, which hit me hard. Having a professional say it, somehow made it more 'real.' Like I'm not just being silly about all of this.

I weighed myself and I'm so unhappy with myself, I've lost only 3 pounds in 2 weeks, how is that even possible?! I have a specific weight in my head. I don't know why, I don't know if that would fix these thoughts to lose more and more and I could finally feel like I could just stop. I don't know what would happen when and if I get there, but that's all I have in my head - it's like a number of comfort.

Numbers in anorexia are like the captain of the ship – they drive that ship forward and control the speed at which it goes. And like the captain of a ship, they will also go down with it.

Anorexia, for me, and a lot of other anorexics I've known, is like an addiction. You're addicted to losing weight; to keep seeing those numbers going down. The adrenaline buzz of seeing them drop, especially when you reach the next set of kilos, or better still, when those pounds lost get to double figures. There is a moment that is so exhilarating... you've done it. You've achieved. However, it never lasts long. Then the next 'goal' is set. You're chasing a buzz, the feeling that you've achieved, that you're good at something... just never quite good enough. I actually once saw a place in the US that treats eating disorders with a similar 12-step program that they use to treat people with substance addictions. I think this is a good idea.

Sunday 19th November 2006

It's my 21st birthday tomorrow! I had to go and have Sunday dinner at my dad's today, which means there will be no birthday meal tomorrow.

I ate my Sunday dinner as quickly as possible so as to not draw any suspicion, but also so that I didn't have to smell and taste all those calories going inside me that I could do nothing about.

I've never felt so full... I honestly thought I was going to explode!

My dad hugged me today and said, "there's hardly anything to hug anymore." Then when I finished my dinner, he was poking on my plate telling me to "eat some vegetables." My step mum told him to leave me alone - thank God - to which he just replied, "Look at her. There's nothing to her!"

I'm meant to be getting my birthday present tomorrow, but my step mum wanted us to come around at 6:00 pm and I'm meant to be seeing the counsellor then, so I had to lie and say we are going for a meal.

I'm getting so exhausted from lying and pretending, it's really horrible and just makes me feel like even more of a shit person.

Wednesday 13th December 2006

This is what my thinking has come to: I cried - more like sobbed - last night because I couldn't figure out the calorie content of my sachet of soup and I NEED to know to figure out to determine what and how much I can eat for the rest of the day!

I'm scared because I know I'm not well, and I don't know what's going to happen. In about a month, I've lost a stone and I have no way of slowing this down. I'm terrified that everyone is going to find out and I can't have that, but it seems there's no alternative or option. I really don't know!

Anorexia is controlled by numbers – and its victims bow down to them. But medical professionals do too. Throughout my history with eating disorders, I have encountered doctors and psychiatrists that work with numbers: weight and body mass index (BMI). If your BMI doesn't 'fit' into the anorexia box, then quite simply in their eyes, you're not anorexic. And so patients will do all that they can to fit into that damned box, however small the box may be - however thin they need to become.

The irony is that by determining anorexia by a number, they are fuelling the eating disorder and weight loss. The worst possible thing a doctor could say to someone with anorexia is that they are not thin enough! *Never* say it. Don't even *think* it. Someone with an eating disorder will sniff that thought out of your head and see it in your eyes. Doctors need to be aware of the words they use when treating patients. I think that words and phrases can be more harmful to patients with eating disorders than we realise.

In most areas of the NHS, you won't be admitted to hospital until your weight is below a certain BMI. Usually it's critically low, where the person is in danger. It's utterly ridiculous. Does someone engaging in daily repeated behaviours, presenting problems associated with that behaviour, not need help? It is still dangerous. It can still kill.

How the NHS deals with eating disorders needs to be reconsidered. Far too much importance is put on numbers – weight and BMI. Eating disorders are a mental illness and the physical food aspect is a response to the thoughts and feelings that drive the illness. To not acknowledge that someone is ill until they reach a certain number is dangerous. That number fuels an already obsessed mind. It will actually make somebody with an eating disorder feel like they need to hit that 'target.' And when they do, it's a damn lot harder to pull them out.

Wednesday 20th December 2006

So... I went to the doctor yesterday. He blatantly thinks I'm lying, or maybe he is completely uninterested.

I told him my heart feels like it's been fluttering, and I feel out of breath when I stand up and his reply was, "You do not look like you have lost enough weight to be having heart problems." He may as well have laughed and said, "You fucking idiot."

So I felt like a complete twat and I was so upset, but I couldn't understand why. I really did feel gutted right down in the pit of my stomach.

Wednesday 27th December 2006

Christmas and a fear of food... not a good combination. I got through Christmas dinner. I just cut it all in to really small pieces and chewed it more than usual - like doing that meant not as much of it would hit me as much on the side, and maybe it would pass through quicker – ridiculous, I know, but It got me through it.

Now all I have in my head is how much I've eaten over Christmas. It's like my brain has gone, 'Right! Back to schedule!' It's just taunting me about what I've eaten and I can't shake it, it's awful. All my hard work has gone down the toilet – unfortunately, not in a literal sense or I might feel a bit happier about it.

Dad was going on about me not eating enough, and you know what? I wish people would just keep their noses out of my fucking business and stop talking about it between themselves.

These past few days has shown me how easy it would be to slip and stuff your face and put all that weight back on. Well, I will NOT let that happen.

My head keeps thinking 'double figures'... below 100 pounds. Surely then, I can say I am not fat? I am not big, I am small. I am 107 pounds now... 8 pounds to go... can I do that without anyone noticing? No one can know this.

Yes, I can do it. A can of Fanta in the morning for sugar. Half a cup of soup sachet in the afternoon. Other half in the evening. I can do this. I can feel better. I can feel small. I can stop this noise in my head. I know I can.

<u>These thoughts in my head</u>

These thoughts in my head

These feelings in my soul

Me focused on another goal

Can I do it? Will I win?

So many things, where to begin

A plan drawn up for me to follow

To try to fill this empty hollow.

<u>My name is Anorexia</u>

My name is Anorexia, let's play a game

Let me just explain, in case you don't know my name

We will plan and organise what we're going to do

Soon I can step back as most will come from you!

Or at least that's what I'll make you think

As my thoughts are yours

I'll push you to the limit from emotions to chores

Then we count calories more obsessively each day

Don't you dare go over or you will have to pay!

Sometimes you'll be tempted to fill that starving hole

But you'll soon be on your knees staring at the toilet bowl

And as your eyes start to stream and the blood rushes to your head

All you'll want to do is curl up in bed

But still we'll keep on going – on and on and on

Only until we're sure that all that food has gone

Or at least until you shake that you can't do it anymore

And have to steady yourself on the bathroom door

With your eyes red and your light head

You stop yourself from falling

At least now you've learned that overeating was appalling

Down and down the scales go - it's really not enough

Looks like I'll have to up this game, I'll have to get more tough

Like any game it will grow tiresome – waiting for it to end

But now we are too attached, and I will not break or bend

You may start to crumble, mentally start to break

But we will carry on my friend, we have to for goodness sake!

We will build on this in time – so much more to say

But for now... my name is Anorexia...

Want to come and play?

Hands Around My Throat

At first, I thought I could keep it under control. Use it as a crutch when I needed it, and that no one would be any the wiser. But it doesn't work that way. Anorexia is like a poison that's drip feeds you. It whispers in your ear that this is going to make you feel so much better; this is going to drown out those thoughts and make you feel like you are in complete control. But after a while, the poison creeps into your veins and you become a shell of your former self, wracked with obsession.

My obsession was the numbers. The numbers going down, hitting a certain number, having a goal to aim for and feeling fantastic when I hit it. I guess it was like my previous sales roles – but this time, it was deadly.

The problem with anorexia is that the more poison that creeps into your veins, the less fantastic you feel when you hit those goals. It stops making you feel better. You don't believe the numbers on the scale. They must be wrong. So are the other 10 scales you've weighed yourself on, because *I know*. It's my body. I know how it feels and I know I've gained weight. It doesn't matter what anyone says; someone with anorexia would be more inclined to believe you if you told them the sky was green. The less someone eats, the more malnourished they get, and the more malnourished they get, the less the brain functions properly. They become irrational, angry, snappy – someone that the people around them may not recognise. They are starving and obsessed. Quite frankly, *nothing* else matters.

Friday 29th December 2006

According to my scales, I'm at the weight I've had in my head all this time. I don't believe it though, so I'm going to weigh myself at Boots, even though I think they are inaccurate - it's the only place I can get a second opinion.

I don't feel like I'm there and I don't look like I'm there... so how can I possibly be there?

I have my psychiatrist appointment in three weeks. That seems so long away with how I'm currently feeling.

I really need something to distract me and focus on, but I feel like I have no ambition, no drive, nothing to aim for... NOTHING TO BE! It's hard to explain.

A friend asked me if I got offered inpatient treatment, would I take it? I doubt I would get offered it as I don't think I'm that bad, but even if I did, I couldn't go in at this weight! I'd be 'the fat one,' surely?!

Am I fat? Or am I thin? Is to win to lose? Or to lose to win?

Wednesday 3rd January 2007

Well happy New Year, I don't think! Rob said to me last night that I'm 'losing my looks'. Yeah, well maybe I am. Do I care though? What does it matter anyway? I'm ugly on the inside so what does the outside matter?

I want the colours back, the spring inside, but everything just feels so damp, cold and clouded.

Rob keeps saying that I need to get better to get my life back on track. Was it ever really on track in the first place? What is on track? That seems so overwhelming right now.

I want to get well for him at the moment. For myself? Sort of, I guess, but what would I be getting better FOR? My life just plods along aimlessly with a gut-wrenching empty feeling in the hollow of my stomach.

The dread of day-to-day living, the way everything feels is too much. The days hurt, I plod through jobs I don't like – this is how I've felt for years and years, why would I want to stop this to gain THAT?

Sunday 7th January 2007

SHIT. SHIT. SHIT. SHIT. My mum rang and I had a message saying, "Katie, ring me," which she never does! So I rang back and she said, "I just wanted to say that it was nice seeing you last night." Straight away, I was like hmmm, as she wouldn't phone and say this normally.

She asked me how my tooth was and my tummy as I've been struggling terribly with my periods, but I'd already told her all this last night. Then she said, "I just wondered because you look like you've lost a bit of weight... are you eating properly?"

So I said, "Yeah, why?" She said, "No, no, I just wondered as I know you're out of work and I was wondering if you had enough money for food and stuff." I hope I did a good enough job in covering this up.

This is NOT GOOD. SHIT.

Saturday 13th January 2007

I'm not feeling too good today, but every inch of my body says I can't eat – I feel so horrendously big. Rob doesn't understand how I can feel this way, but my brain feels somehow blocked to rational thoughts. I filled out forms today online for diet pill samples; whether they come or not, I don't know.

I'm out of control, I know that. I'm fucked up, I know that too, but I'm too tired and I cannot fight every thought that comes in my head anymore. Plus, those thoughts are MY thoughts now, I can't distinguish the two - they are the same voice: mine.

I still feel too big, I'm too much over 7 stone. Every time I have a thought about eating, it's like a big black curtain comes down on it and I can't push the thought any further to make the thought become an action, because it just gets pushed from my mind with a knot in my stomach as if it's a disgusting option. Not an option at all.

I'm trapped.

I need to lose, I just have to. I need to get to a little lower, just a little bit lower.

Thursday 18th January 2007

There really is nothing else to say at this point, apart from the fact that my life is a fucking mess.

I've never felt like I did last night, I actually felt really unsafe in myself. It was a horrible place, like I actually felt like I was going mad! I actually feel like I'm on the edge of a full-blown breakdown. I just want God to take me away, and I don't actually believe in God... maybe that's the problem?

I was actually praying last night, 'please, please just take me.' I've never even prayed before but that's actually how desperate I feel. This is NOT how my life was supposed to be! I had dreams and aspirations and I just feel like I'm letting myself down.

I'm hurting Rob and I'm going to hurt everyone else if they find out, and I don't think I can cope with that. I can't even cope with a normal day. I wouldn't wish this feeling on anyone else ever.

I DON'T KNOW WHAT TO DO! HELP ME!

Friday 19th January 2007

I feel like my life is crumbling around me and I'm just watching it fall and no matter how much I run and wear myself out trying to catch it and put it all back together and stop further damage, something stops me – my brain – I'm too tired and helpless, so I just let it fall, close my eyes and pray to God that it stops.

By this point, I was living on a knife's edge. I felt like I was watching my life happen around me. People moved and spoke and got on with their lives, and I just stood in the middle of it all. I was invisible, watching all the movement, so much movement that I just couldn't keep up. I didn't want to keep up and I didn't want to be part of it anymore.

I was a shell. A hollow being. Literally empty of food, but also empty of life. Just moving from one thing to the next. When needed, I acted like I thought I should; but then I just reverted into myself, consumed by calories and numbers. The scale no longer had any elation attached to it, just relief that I wasn't getting bigger. I needed to be smaller. As small as humanly possible so that I barely existed, or not at all. Preferably, without anyone noticing, which amazingly up until this point had been a successful endeavor.

Looking back, I think they knew. I think people find it hard to confront or ask the question. Especially when they have no prior knowledge of anorexia and what it involves. It's easy to think that things like that only happen to other people. To celebrities who want to be thin. Why on earth would I do such a thing? I mean, how are you supposed to ask someone if they are starving themselves?

Wednesday 24th January 2007

So the day finally came for my first psychiatric appointment... what a load of shit!

Granted, he has referred me to the Queen Elizabeth Hospital to an eating disorder specialist, but apart from that, I came out feeling like utter crap!

He asked me whether I thought what I am doing is sensible; that I seem like a sensible girl, so do I think this is what I should be doing?!

He said I am not 'diagnostic,' or in other words, I am not 'textbook' anorexic (that's after telling me that I had lost 15% of my weight). But he did kindly tell me that I need to eat more?!

NO. SHIT. SHERLOCK!

I don't know how long it will before I see this specialist. Also due to me being out of work and Rob's hours being cut, we can't afford to live here, and we had the end of tenancy notice today.

What am I going to do?

As I said before (but it's worth saying again), *never* tell someone with anorexia they are not 'diagnostic'. *Please,* don't ever tell them they are not 'anorexic' yet, but they will be if they carry on. It's like waving a red flag in front of a bull.

Wednesday 31st January 2007

Well I had an operation today. With all the eating disorder stuff, I don't think I've even spoken about it in this diary!

I went to see if I have endometriosis as I've been suffering terribly for years with my periods, even after all the weight I've lost, they have never stopped. I do have endometriosis. After seven years of fighting doctors and being told from 14 that 'I'll grow out of it,' it's finally been confirmed.

On top of the operation, we're likely to be homeless soon and on top of that, I'm trying to deal with myself. I'm so utterly exhausted. I feel like I don't even care what happens anymore.

Monday 19th February 2007

I feel a bit fucked up at the moment. My step mum told me that dad had been texting a 15-year-old girl off the internet. I know it's not the case, but I can't help wondering if he's ever looked at me in that way? And then I feel so horrible even thinking that, but it really makes my head feel screwed up. I like to try and think she's lying, but with all the other things that I know and have been told, why would she? It can't all be lies, can it? I just like to bat it away from my mind and pretend it's not there. It's the only thing I can do to preserve my sanity... ha, sanity, what's that?!

I realise now that I was dealing with so much and I had every right to feel how I did. I'd had to move home after an operation; I'd just found out that I had endometriosis and that this can lead to difficulties conceiving; I was struggling with the news that my dad was texting a 15-year-old girl; all while trying to battle crippling anorexic thoughts. But at the time, I really believed that I was pathetic, that I was ruining my relationship and that I had nothing going for me.

Rob was no help. He was never in and he was smoking weed like cigarettes. I felt totally alone. But I couldn't see this at the time. People told me I could do better than him, but I didn't want better. I loved him very much and he was the one I wanted to be with. As they say: love is blind.

Wednesday 28th February 2007

I have been for my follow-up appointment for the endometriosis. It was supposed to be the consultant who did my operation, but it was a man who literally just read me the letter that I already got in the post.

Rob doesn't understand why I'm so anxious and upset about this... I feel like asking him how he would feel if he had adhesions growing on his balls which caused immense pain, terrible bleeding and could probably mess up the one thing in the world he wanted – children – while being told by people that it may be a good idea to start thinking about trying for children, while hiding from everyone that I'm battling an eating disorder, so that isn't even an option, and I'm ironically screwing up the chances of having children even more, all by myself.

I HATE ME. I HATE ME SO MUCH!

What am I? Nothing.

What do I do? Nothing.

All I want it to be fucking something.

I'm stuck. Stuck. Fucking stuck.

All I want to do right now is put a blade to my wrist.

If someone broke in the house right now with a gun and tried to shoot me I wouldn't even fight.

It would be a godsend.

What do you do when no one can take away your pain?

What do you do when it feels there's nothing left to gain?

How do you solve a problem when you don't know where to start?

And how do you solve problems when life is tearing at your heart?

How can you expect love and care if you don't give it out?

And how do you give it to those you love when all you feel is doubt?

When everything good is crumbling, please tell me – how do you put it right?

When the one thing you need to do seems totally out of sight.

Wednesday 7th March 2007

I'm still waiting to hear back from the hospital to see what's going to happen in regards to help. I haven't heard anything, so I'm thinking I can't be all that bad then. I have been trying to make a conscious decision to eat, but I totally freak out at the thought of gaining so much as a pound.

I think it's harder as time goes on because so much time and effort goes into losing - it's all-consuming. It's not just about losing weight and gaining weight. It would be so much easier to gain weight than to keep losing it, and all of this work I've put in to getting to these goals would just be wasted... another thing that I'd be giving up without finishing?

I've been thinking about that and how I feel like things I've done have either not been completed or just been bettered by someone else. For example, when I was starting my National Vocational Qualification at the nursery, dad told me that 'monkeys could do my job.' But one of my stepsisters was working in the same place doing the same jobs as part of her teacher training placement, and that was ok because it was to lead to bigger and better things... I gave it up. Then my nail course – no one has really taken any notice of the fact that I'm even doing it, let alone asked me how it's going. But my step mum wanted a change of career and did her beauty training at the same time, and is starting her own business and everyone thinks it's great – better than me.

I apply for mental health nursing and am rejected. My other stepsister has started her nursing training – another failure.

Then there's just the little things. I loved drama so much and dad didn't speak to me for ages when I started it at college – I ended up giving it up. I know there were a lot of other factors linked to that, but that was still a big one. I felt like I wasn't good enough before I even started.

The first time I had a poem published, I showed my dad and my step mum, and she just said how depressing it was. So I never showed anyone else after that.

Before I started on this eating disorder path, I was having some photo shoots and doing a little bit of modelling – Rob hated it. We nearly split up over it and so I gave that up too.

It just goes on, and I guess this is how I feel about me and my life – nothing is good enough. I'm not good enough. I make wrong choices and everyone does better. Looks better. Is better. And that's just the way it is.

Looking back is a funny thing. It's amazing how you can connect the dots. As I sit here today, writing this, I become almost uncomfortably aware of how things follow us around in different forms.

This idea of 'completion' is still something that I struggle with. I now have a small self-made creative business. It's my drive, my focus and a huge part of who I am. When I receive orders, I feel a sense of urgency to complete them there and then. I don't stop until it's done, and the faster I can do it, the better. I'm constantly battling with it. I also feel the need to train or complete some academic goal to be worthy.

It is something that has followed me wherever I have gone, and along every path I have taken. I realise now that it all stems from this time in my life. Knowing how to manage your demons – in whatever form they take – or at least being conscious of what's happening, is half the battle. But it can take such an awfully long time to realise this.

At this point in my diaries, I was so obsessed and consumed by numbers that in the top right-hand corner of every entry is my weight in pounds. A daily confirmation of my worth, dictated by those numbers. I may as well have been a number because that was all I existed for. I never felt good. I don't think I really ever had a good day, but it made that tiny bit of microscopic difference if the numbers told me what I wanted to see. It almost gave me hope in the pit of my stomach. I felt that I was 'completing'; that I was achieving a personal goal that no one could take away from me. This goal didn't matter to anyone else, no one else would even understand it. But I did. I understood. It wasn't something someone else could do better or even compete with. I was a champion of this and that was the way it was going to stay.

Thursday 26th April 2007

I had my first appointment with the specialist on Monday, and wow... it was intense! I was asked what seemed like every question under the sun about my whole life, even down to whether I was born prematurely or not, and when I said yes, they asked loads of questions about that too! They took blood and I have to go back on the 8th to find out what is going to happen...

Monday 30th April 2007

So I did it, I reached the ultimate goal. This is what I've been striving for, what I thought I'd never do, that I'd never be 'one of those.' The funny thing is, I still don't...

Was I really expecting to hit this point and feel like I'd made it? Like I could stop now? Was that ever really going to happen?

It's funny, I lie in bed at night thinking about how shitty this all is, how tired I am, paranoid that I might have a heart attack or something. Thinking that I don't want this shit; that I want normality, I want kids, a job, to train... but then I get up every morning and do the same damned thing over again. It's so confusing, it's like being two different people in one body that I don't even want to be in.

I'm a little calmer today (after making myself sick three times and cutting - all the completely normal things that people do to calm down, of course!)

I'm 96.8 pounds today and I think I feel slightly better as its moving further away from 100 pounds. Do I really want to end up in hospital though? Is that really going to prove anything to myself? Oh yes, I forgot, it means that I will be a 'good anorexic.'

I just paused before I wrote that... like, I really didn't want to write it but that's what diaries are for right?! I just don't like to think of myself as having 'anorexia.' It kind of makes me cringe inside. I just can't see myself as being 'anorexic' and plus, no professional has actually said the term outright to me, so I guess it leaves room for me to think that maybe I'm not.

I'm so hungry, soooooo fucking hungry. I keep thinking about takeaways, but I absolutely can't.

Food drives anorexics (or at least me) crazy. It simply isn't true that they hate food and are never hungry. Even in hospital, we all cried over the meals, the snacks, the glasses of blackcurrant juice and those Fortisips (which to be fair, did deserve real tears). But secretly, we were all mad for the evening bowl of muesli because it was so incredibly sweet. Even if we hated eating it, there's no denying that deep down, we craved it (and many of us went on to buy it after discharge).

I remember that I once spent two hours online, looking at a McDonalds menu, picking what I'd eat, what it felt like, what it smelled like and, God forbid, what it tasted like. Forget virtual reality; all I needed was a starving body, a starving mind and a McDonalds' menu and I was lost in a world of french fries, hamburgers and melted cheese.

Wednesday 9th May 2007

Well I had my appointment and according to their scales I'm under the goal weight I had set for myself. The doctor wants me to do the day care program, which I understand is Monday -Friday and you go in the morning and come home in the afternoon/evening.

I was very surprised since the last time he was just talking about group and individual therapy, so I really wasn't expecting anything as intense as this to be honest.

I don't know how I feel about it. I am terrified by all the meals, etc. but at the same time, if I don't cooperate with this, then I'm probably going to end up as an inpatient and I really don't want that. So I suppose I'll just wait until I have to meet with the manager of the day care program and find out what will happen.

Apparently, there's a three-month waiting list anyway!

Thursday 15th May 2007

Well, I went to the day care unit yesterday to meet the manager. Rob came with me, bless him. When she came and got me, she asked him to wait there and left him on the sofa with all the girls. He said he just sat there staring at the bin - that did make me laugh!

I felt soooooooo uncomfortable walking in there though, every part of me was saying that there was no way that I needed to go to this sort of place. You know, it's just the sort of thing you see on the TV or that hear about in a book about someone else's life of their struggle with an eating disorder – not the sort of place that I GO! I'm going to feel like an utter idiot – I feel so weak.

Plus, you should see the menus! I mean, this program is Monday-Friday 8am-4pm and the food they cram into that time is absolutely ridiculous! I really don't know if I want to go, but Rob says I have to.

Breakfast is toast with jam or whatever AND cereal! It will be 'fat bread' as well, because they're not exactly going to give me my Weight Watchers, are they?!

This means that with the breakfast alone, I'd be eating more than what I'm eating on a whole normal day, which means I'm going to put on weight like a mother fucker and I will be a complete fat ass in 0.2 seconds and all of this will have been for nothing.

I don't know what I was expecting... I guess just not that much food! I've never eaten as much as what's on those menus between 8am-4pm on a normal day in my life, let alone at the moment. I can't bear the thought of it. It makes me feel sick and I don't know if this is what I want.

I need to get lower first, then maybe I'd feel like I could do it... but I can never tell Rob that. There's a waiting list anyway, so I guess I've still got time.

The further into Anorexia you travel, the more it grabs you by the throat. The grip tightens. The pressure to lose more weight increases and the thoughts and obsessions are out of this world.

The more you lose, the more the need to lose intensifies. Those once far off goals have come and gone. What was once the ultimate thin goal becomes 'fat'. And it's never, *ever* enough.

This is why anorexia is one of the deadliest mental illnesses. Once it grabs hold, it does not let go. Like an addiction: the more you do, the more you need, the more you take, the more of a chance you have of overdosing and dying, but you have to keep doing more because those initial hits just don't even touch the surface anymore. And those initial numbers were so horrendously big that you need to lose so much more to be as humanly far away from them as possible. Even if you were a wisp of air, it would be too much. The only thing that would satisfy you would be to simply not exist at all.

Wednesday 16th May 2007

I officially realised yesterday that I must be fucked up.

I worked out that if I can lose just a few more pounds, then my BMI would be where I want it, and as I realised that, I had a feeling of absolute exhilaration. But only for a few seconds. I attempted to put my logical brain on and thought, 'why the fuck is that good?!' Below that is classed as emaciation. It's heart attack status, it's inpatient material, so why the hell on a logical level am I aiming for that? Am I some sort of fucked up attention seeker? I don't think so. I mean, the last thing I want to do is flaunt this, but then why?

I tell myself this so often, but then the importance of all those numbers just overrides it. Does that mean I want an eating disorder more than I want to get better? I hope not, that's not what I want to want...

Monday 21st May 2007

Well! Yesterday was a very, very awkward day!

I went to my nan's and she stockpiled food on me to bring home while saying, "I won't let you waste away you! We don't want you being anorexic, do we?!"

It totally threw me that, of all people, she would be the first to say it because, if I'm honest, I wouldn't have even thought she'd know what anorexia is!

I kept hearing them quietly talking when I went out of the room too. She said I was a bag of bones and I was in my 'hiding' clothes too! So this makes me absolutely dread seeing dad, as by the time I see him next, I won't have seen him for three or four weeks.

I've noticed that I've been paying more attention to chewing my food - the little food I have, anyway. I feel like if there are not 'bits' left, then it will somehow digest quicker. Either that or I've just started chewing it and spitting it out altogether. That way I don't even have to worry about it, although that's not necessarily true as I'm sure that even by chewing some, calories would be consumed somehow – or is that just complete craziness?!

I found out that the waiting list for day care is two to three months, and my appointments with the psychiatrist have gone from every two weeks to every four weeks, apparently?! This has really confused me and yet again, made me feel like I'm not bad enough. Not worthy of help or treatment. Clearly, I'm okay on my own then for the next four weeks to completely self-destruct.

Reading this back, my blood boils. My BMI dangerously low. It was quite clear that I was still losing weight quickly and that I was struggling with depression. I'd finally taken the plunge and sought help. Yet, I was still on a two to three month waiting list and my psychiatry appointments were cut from once a fortnight to once a month! The anorexia screams, 'See, I told you you're not thin enough! You've failed again.' And so, I was left for longer without help. And when my appointment eventually came around, I was more entrenched, less willing, less rational.

It is well-documented that there is a shortage of beds for people struggling with eating disorders, and that often people are not getting the help they need until they reach a critically low BMI. New research published by the *Guardian* shows that eating disorder admissions have doubled in the last six years (the number of admissions peaked at 13,885 in April 2017, up from 7,260 in 2011). The timescales and services are not good enough. This time is vital. The longer you leave someone with an eating disorder, the further they fall and the harder it is to get them out.

Much like an addiction – they really do have such similar traits – the more an addict uses, the harder it is to pull them out; the harder it is for them to accept treatment; and the harder it is not to fall back into the habit, because the brain has relied on it for so long.

Don't think it's easy. Don't think we just lose weight because we can't eat, or don't want to eat. It's a sustained effort to keep pushing on and on. All the while, feeling weaker, more depressed and starving hungry. Every second of every day. An obsession with numbers and calories and working out what we need to lose to reach yet another goal. It's exhausting. Utterly exhausting. But we keep going because it pushes us to. That voice: 'You're fat. You're revolting. You will feel better if you get to that number. You can do better. You can lose more'. And then the odd friendly nudge: 'Look how well you're doing,' just to keep us going that little bit more. It becomes a crutch, a best friend, a 'better the devil you know' way of living.

Friday 25th May 2007

Well yesterday escalated quickly... Rob announced to me that we owed council tax from the old flat. He had tried to sort it but failed, and bailiffs were on their way to take our stuff! I had to borrow the money AGAIN – God knows what we owe now, and we still owe the bailiffs £500 next month. I spoke to mum and she started saying that she wanted to come over and help me work out a plan for a budget. By this point, I was so stressed, tired, and ill, and my nan had already mentioned earlier to her four times that I look anorexic. She asked why and I couldn't say those words, I hate that word, so I just said, 'What did nan say to you?' Mum said, 'Nothing...' and then I heard the pause and I heard the penny drop and she said, 'What? Anorexic? Is that what you are?'

I said yes. She asked how long and what I weigh, and it wasn't nearly as bad as I was expecting. I told her that I felt stupid and she said that I shouldn't because it's a medical problem. She said she always felt stupid about her cleaning, but that she felt she had to do it or it really stressed her out. Funny as we've never spoken about that, but it was a little moment in a strange way. She even offered to come to appointments with me and that was really nice and a gesture that I wasn't expecting. I thought people would just tell me to get a grip and to just eat some food and that I was being ridiculous.

She is going to tell my nan too, which I agreed to very reluctantly - only because she already knows and also, I owe her money and she thinks I have a job still. I feel uncomfortable about people knowing but, I don't know, maybe it's a good thing.

Sunday 27th May 2007

OH. MY. GOD. I thought yesterday was bad and stressful? It was NOTHING compared to today!

First, mum came around and she looked at me and started crying because of my weight.

Then Nany came looking upset. AND THEN, all of a sudden, out of the blue, I get a text message from my step mum saying, 'I'm coming around, I think we need to talk.'

My brain went into PANIC – mum and Betty had LITERALLY just found out. They were both sat in my flat, very upset. I felt awkward beyond belief and wanted the ground to swallow me, and now this. Right now.

I text back, 'What, is everything ok?' and I get back, 'I'm more worried about you after the conversation I just had with Rob.' WHAT?! He's done this to me today? Now? At this moment? WHY? I text Rob, who was at work, and all he could manage to text back was, 'I didn't mean to – I'm sorry.'

My step mum turned up and she started crying too... I'm standing there, thinking is bloody ridiculous! All of a sudden, she's on the phone with my dad saying, 'You need to get here now - she's like a skeleton.' NO. NO. NO. NO. NO!

So in my tiny lounge, there was me, mum, my nan, my step mum and my dad (who at first, apparently, wasn't coming because he was 'going to have a drink' – my dad isn't a big drinker to begin with and then when he did show up, he was spruced up to nines with aftershave on, the lot, so I really wouldn't be surprised if he's up to something or having an affair).

He waltzed in and announced to the room, including my mum, that he, "Needs to speak to his daughter... alone." He took me into the bedroom and my heart was banging, I've been dreading this moment for so long and I couldn't believe everyone was here finding out at the same time! He said that it's all because I need a job, I need a focus and that I need to pull myself out of it.

Then, on the other hand, he was being all like he understood – to be honest, it was a really contradictory and confusing conversation.

As it turns out, what had happened was that Rob had told his friend about it all back in February, then after the bailiff incident, he texted him... only he sent it to my step mum instead, who is one down on the phone book!

Me and mum talked, and she spoke about all the obsessive traits in the family and while her and my step mum talked about my dad, she mentioned the overdoses too. It's crazy, so much came out today, and so much has happened in such a short space of time!

My head feels absolutely screwed up and I don't know how to feel or think about anything. I'm just so tired.

Wednesday 30th May 2007

My stepsisters came over yesterday for five hours, which was actually really nice. We were talking about all the stuff to do with dad exposing himself to school girls. Apparently, one girl he followed and did it down an alley! He was supposedly charged and on probation for two years.

It makes me feel physically sick... pedophilia. That's what it is, surely?! My dad?!

I can't even bear to think about it. I also can't believe that his first instinct the other day was to say, 'I'm going for a drink.' The situation wasn't something he felt the need to come straight here for? Mum has rung me every single night. Dad hasn't even text me. I just don't get it, and I certainly don't get him. He makes my head feel so fucked.

A major part of anorexia is secrecy. The secrecy is what's comforting. It's a crutch, something of your own, something to cling to. But as a secret, it's even more deadly.

Much like the self-harming, it's not something you want to shout from the rooftops or to divulge the details of. You formulate a plan, a routine, a method. Anorexia is extremely strategic. It's something that takes time and constant monitoring. No one else can be involved or it will mess with that plan. Too many cooks spoil the broth (no pun intended), and this delicate mixture cannot be ruined.

You think others will make you feel ridiculous; they won't understand (how could they). The worst thought in the world is trying to explain why you are starving yourself to someone who doesn't have a clue. Especially when you don't even understand it yourself.

Looking back, it's glaringly obvious to me why I felt the need to do this. It gave me comfort – everything was so out of control in all other parts of my life. But at the time, if you'd had asked me why I was doing what I was doing, I simply wouldn't have been able to tell you. It was too confusing and complicated. It was overwhelming. I wouldn't have known where to start to process it all. And the longer it goes on, the more the brain is staved until it's not even possible anymore.

Telling people is hard. So hard. You don't want to let them down. You don't want to have to explain. You don't want them to think badly of you when you already feel so bad about yourself.

However, the cold-hard fact is that you need people to get better – whether it's family, a friend, a doctor, a nurse, a psychiatrist… somewhere along the line, you need someone. People have to find out. If they didn't find out, what would happen? Most probably wouldn't be here. If I'd had no input from other human beings, I'd be dead.

It wasn't possible for me to just carry on with no-one finding out. Yes, the way it happened was horrendous – with everyone at once – and yes, I hated the fact people knew. It still surprises me that I managed to hide it for that long – but it had to happen. And I do hope that if there is anyone reading this book that is still hiding it, living with these daily secrets, that you can read this and understand that it will be hard. There is no point in me lying, it's like giving away your crutch and then people watching as you attempt to walk. But it's so necessary. And it does get easier. You may also get a reaction that you weren't expecting. It may just lessen the load. You don't know until you take the plunge. And sometimes, you just have to plunge.

TREATMENT TREADMILL

Treating anorexia is difficult. And the first time is the hardest. You don't know what to expect, or what will be expected of you. You wonder if anyone will like you, or how the doctors and nurses are going to be. But the one thing you *do* know is that you are there for them to take away your crutch and to put on weight.

For me, and most of the patients I have spoken to over my many admissions, day care is actually harder to deal with than being an inpatient. You would think it would be better to go home in the evening than to stay somewhere without any friends or family. At least you still have the freedom to do as you please once you get home, right? Wrong.

In reality, you eat the same as the inpatients, you have the same group sessions, you talk about the same things and the same crutch is taken away - but then you have to hobble home without that crutch. You're in pain. You arrive exhausted, knowing that you are expected to carry on with their plan, but without the confines of those walls and without the nurses monitoring you. It's on *your* shoulders. It's extremely difficult and a large proportion of people in day care go on to become inpatients.

Doctors, campaigners and MPs have warned that the alarming increase in admissions over the last six years indicates that outpatient treatment isn't working effectively, resulting in more people in need of hospital admission. I can relate to this personally. When I look back at my time as an outpatient, I heard things like, "You're not anorexic yet, but you will be if you continue." This only results in someone feeling inadequate, and making those admission numbers feel like a goal to hit.

Day care would probably have a better success rate if it was offered to people earlier in the illness. Unfortunately, from what I have seen over the years, most day care patients are too far down the line for it to work. In my opinion, they also need separate facilities for day care and inpatients. Anorexia is very competitive by nature and this can be a dangerous mix.

Tuesday 10th July 2007

I started day care yesterday. It's so hard and I'm only on day two. I'm on 'introductory portions,' so breakfast at the moment is a bowl of cereal with a glass of orange juice and then a piece of toast and a cup of tea. Then lunch, for example, today was two sausages in a sauce, two potato things and peas, but the amount will go up and I'll also have to have a snack twice a day.

Yesterday I was so upset because I walked in and I felt so unbelievably fat. There are only three other day patients, the rest are inpatients.

I was talking today to one of the day patient girls who is SO thin and she has just come out of seven months of inpatient treatment! She told me how fat she feels and how thin I look in comparison, and that completely blew my mind. I looked at myself and at her and I literally can't see how she would think that? Is that what she was thinking about me too? Am I really not seeing the truth? That is scary... I kind of felt like she was just saying it, or that's what the voice in my head told me but I was left with a strange feeling after that. I just couldn't make sense of it.

Yesterday though, when I got home, I only had a couple of plain biscuits and then I made myself sick. I went back today and thought I'd actually be honest, and when I told the dietician she said, "Well, if you're going to do that then I have to ask why you're really here?"

What?! I'd been there a day and I'd eaten more in those hours than I would in a whole day. I couldn't cope with going home and eating more, I honestly couldn't have done it. I ate all of what they put in front of me and then she said that?! I can't win.

Someone told me if you refuse to eat, they threaten you with discharge but that seems so harsh!

I tried to explain to the dietician and she said, "We'll see how the two-weeks-in-period goes because you might get to the end of it and it just might not be the right time for you." Is there ever a right time?! Give me a bloody chance!

I was told I could have three dislikes. I told her I didn't like the three cereals on the list for tomorrow's breakfast choices, which I genuinely don't, and asked if I could swap to another one from the other days. I was told I couldn't because it would set all the other patients off... well then, why the hell give me three dislikes if I'm telling you I dislike it and I have to eat it anyway?! The answer to that was that it's all about 'challenges.' If I were well and 'normal,' would I 'challenge' myself to eat food that I don't like?! Nope!

Then again, she said, "You do want to be here, don't you?" I just said yes, but it made me feel so crappy and I feel crap enough as it is anyway! Why keep making those comments? And does anyone really want to be there? Does anyone there roll out of bed with excitement knowing what they will be doing today? It's a battle, and this was my first attempted step, and now I'm just thinking I can't even get that right. Maybe I'm supposed to be really enthusiastic about it?

I haven't even been there three days and I'm already questioning it because of all that.

So, not a great start.

Tuesday 24th July 2007

I haven't written for a while. I've not known what to write, I guess, as I just feel so confused and lost.

I haven't gone to day care today – I decided I just needed a day off from the whole thing. From comments that keep getting made that I keep questioning, the food, everything. Not that it matters, as I highly doubt I will be there within a week or two anyway. That's pretty much guaranteed as my weight is the same as when I went in and I'm not eating enough at home, so in their eyes I will no doubt either not want to get better or I'm simply not trying.

Yes, I could come home and eat more - but even if I did, I physically cannot resist the urge to make myself sick. Does that mean I don't want to get well? In my eyes, I do want to get well. As in I don't want to be going through this day in day out anymore, but I also don't want to add weight on. It's not clean cut and straight forward and surely that's the whole eating disorder anyway? But sometimes it feels it needs to be a clean-cut line there. You want to get well, or you don't. But this is so far from black and white. It's a whole grey and terribly murky area. The whole reason I am not coming home and eating 'riskier foods' is that I don't want to gain weight. End of story. But then if I didn't have an eating disorder, I wouldn't feel that way, and the reason I feel that way is the reason that I'm there, right?!

Again, I saw the doctor that I really don't like yesterday and his words were, "You know, you really need to start challenging yourself because if day care doesn't work for you then you really don't have that many other options. There is inpatient, but I don't know whether that's really right for you or whether you really need it."

My brain translation: "You know, you really need to start challenging yourself because if day care doesn't work for you then you may as well give up. There is inpatient, but I don't think you're nearly as bad as anyone else. You're a lot bigger, so you don't need that kind of help." This man knows how I feel, he knows I've been feeling suicidal, he knows about the self-harming - which has been getting worse again - but those are his word choices. Back to feeling like I just can't do anything right.

It's so confusing. On one hand, I keep getting told about my low BMI, and on the other hand, I get told that if this doesn't work, I don't really have any other options for help because I don't really need it. And this is within an eating disorder unit. On one hand, that makes me angry as that's not going to help anyone ever. On the other hand, I'm totally more inclined to believe it as these are people that help people like me day in day out.

Friday 27th July 2007

As predicted, I have been told that if there is no improvement by next week then I will be discharged to outpatients. Helpful. My head is in pieces.

I will be gutted in a way, as I love being with all the other girls - but I'm supposed to gain 0.5 kilograms a week and I've gained 0.4 kilograms in three weeks.

I wish I could do what they want and what they are asking me to do and feel ok with it, but I don't and it annoys the crap out of me as much as I'm sure it does them. The only difference is that I have to live in this hell hole and feel like I'm being pulled from every direction with no other real outside support. Where is my excuse for a life going?

Sunday 5th August 2007

I was discharged. No shock there. I just couldn't do what they wanted. Eat all that food there all day and come home and eat more on my own.

We kind of agreed that I need to deal with the psychological issues before I can give up the eating disorder. Even though to be honest, I did think that was what I going for but it just felt so much about the food.

I have been seeing a psychologist, but it was only for a limited time. I only have two more sessions and then I will be put on another waiting list to see someone else which will apparently be about four weeks. So... I'm back on my ass, on my own again.

I was upset leaving since I made friends and I got used to being around people in the day, rather than on my own, and now I'm just back to square one.

Thursday 30th August 2007

So, I've lost even more weight; I don't think I really even have any feelings about this anymore. Rob has been away for a week in Ibiza and it's been tough. I've literally just let go of any fight I had. What's the use? After an appointment with the psychologist, I was told I needed to go back to the hospital and see the doctor because they were worried about me. He said, "Well, it seems you probably will have to be an inpatient but there are no beds at the moment."

He asked if I had any physical symptoms. I told him I ache, I feel shaky a lot and tired and sometimes I feel tight-chested and he said, "Ok, we will just see how it goes." Then straight after, I saw the dietician. We don't seem to have got on from the start and I always dread seeing her.

She said, "You are knocking on inpatients' door. You have two options; either you make changes at home or when there is a bed, you will have to come in. If you come in, you know it's not like day care, don't you? You won't be able to go home until your BMI is quite a bit higher and that's not fair on Rob, is it?" She asked me why I was doing it. Was I doing it for attention? Was it so that Rob wouldn't leave me? I felt so angry because it's not any of those things!

Apparently, she gets frustrated with me because I seem 'ambivalent' and not motivated or willing to change. Am I seriously the only person here that isn't motivated to put weight on? I can't take feeling like I'm being made to feel guilty by someone that is supposed to help. It makes me feel like they are right and it's all true and I end up even more confused.

I know that in a way, she's saying that the only person that can change this is me - but I CAN'T. How do I explain any more clearly without seeming like an ambivalent cow? Isn't this what they are there for? Don't they recognise this in people? Or am I literally the only one who's completely reluctant to weight gain?

My blood boils looking back on some of my treatments over the years (not just for the anorexia, but with other doctors in psychiatry, and even GPs). How could the dietician have thought that those were appropriate words: that I was 'hard work.' More than one doctor has told me that I can talk about big events in my life like I'm talking about the weather. I detach very easily and with all the chaos in my mind and the anorexic voice screaming in my head, I probably did come across as ambivalent. But that doesn't mean that I wasn't worthy of treatment. They didn't need to ask whether I did it for attention, or to force a reaction from me by saying that it wasn't fair on my partner, whom I was already feeling extremely guilty about.

Don't get me wrong: for an anorexic, nothing you say will be right. In some of the diary entries, I can see that I took what they said out of context. But not always. There are trained medical professionals out there who say things that they really shouldn't. That is not okay.

Patients don't always tell their doctors everything. Did any of them know what had gone on in my past? Some of the things that had happened not long before my admission to day care? Sure, I didn't tell them. But at the same time, professionals that work in this field need to be so careful. Unfortunately, I think that some professionals stop seeing the patients as individuals. They hear the same things day in day out, they forget that the feelings and circumstances behind each person is different.

There are some diamonds. Really, there are. But just one comment can make or break you. Especially comments like the one about it not being fair to Rob, when I was already guilt-ridden. I may have seemed hard-faced and ambivalent, but I had been made that way over the years. And I was terrified that you were taking away my crutch.

Saturday 22nd September 2007

I'm writing this in bed, in the unit. Yes – inpatient unit. I was admitted two days ago.

I never actually thought it would come to this for some reason. I really don't feel like I should be here. I feel so much fatter than everyone else. I just can't get my head around the fact that I can possibly be as bad as them.

I always thought if I got to a certain weight, surely then I would feel like I didn't need to lose any more weight, but honestly, I don't think even if I got to 2 pounds that I would be satisfied.

It's hard in here. Lunch is the hardest for me. I never thought I'd cry about having to eat. When needed, I kind of grit my teeth and bear it, but you don't realise just how messed up your thinking is and how hard it truly is until a full plate of food is put under your nose.

I have to be honest, and that part of me is glad that I'm here. I was so drained from all the making myself sick, and I had no control over it or myself. My body was aching so much. I was walking with cramps everywhere.

On the other hand though, I already miss feeling hungry and the euphoria that it gives. I hate, hate, hate being full, but I know that I was never going to be satisfied. I know that I would have carried on until I died or I was sectioned. I know that nothing and nobody would have stopped me from doing what I was doing. Something was going to happen at some point, and so I need to try and hold to the fact that I've done the right thing.

It's strange when people visit. It makes it seem more real. It also makes me feel very ashamed.

If I can get through this though, then me and Rob will be happier as I won't be obsessed by all of this anymore.

Tuesday 25th September 2007

I can't do this.

I've just stood by the toilet for five minutes, tormenting myself whether to attempt to be sick, even though it won't achieve anything anyway since I ate so long ago. I have so much anxiety about not being able to do it, especially today. It's almost unbearable and it's seriously getting to me. On the one hand, I'm glad that I can't do it like I was doing before I came in, but on the other hand, not being able to do it at all and eating so much - I can't deal with it.

I've been cutting just to try and get rid of some of the anxiety and frustration I feel, as I feel like I have no outlet for it now at all.

My thoughts are a mess. When I'm doing all the eating disorder behaviours, I hate it and I can't live with it... but then when I don't, I feel like I'm going to go mad and feel like I can't live without it and the not being able to do it is quite possibly worse than just doing it, even though logically, that's not the way I want to live. That statement is filled with so many contradictions and that's why my head feels like such a mess all the time.

It can make it worse sometimes, being in a unit like this, because it's so easy for everyone to rub off on one another.

Sunday 30th September 2007

Weigh-day tomorrow. I'm dreading it.

I had an awful day today. I ate my lunch but by the end of it, I was literally forcing it down because I was so uncomfortably full. I literally felt sick and like I was going to explode. My heart was going absolutely crazy and when I'd finished it, all I could think about was making myself sick or getting the hell out of the hospital. I can't explain how intense the feeling was - I literally couldn't deal with it. I looked around and there were no staff sitting in the lounge like there is supposed to be after meal times, so I went as quick as I could to the toilets around the corner, but I was so full of adrenaline and shaking so much that I couldn't even throw anything up and within a minute, they came and got me. I said that I wanted to go home. He said that he would get the doctor for me and that I'd either be discharged, sent on leave or read the mental health act (i.e. sectioned), and he didn't know which it would be.

I took my chances. While I was waiting, I spoke to Rob who said that if I left then he would move back in with his parents. And so that is the only reason that I am still here. It's at times like this that I realise how strong our relationship is. I didn't realise how strong my feelings are until someone is trying to take it away. It's awful.

Friday 5th October 2007

I kind of realised this evening how this voice in my head will literally take any opportunity to come out in full force.

I had an appointment today about my endometriosis, so I had to get up, have breakfast with a member of staff on my own (which was awkward as hell) and they had to come with me, but they obviously had to wait in the waiting room.

Half way through the scan, I was told that I needed to go and empty my bladder. This was obviously an opportunity I could not miss, so I made myself sick, went back into the room to have the rest of the scan, then came out and did it again before going back to the nurse.

The thing is, though, I did it on autopilot. Like it was logical, like it made sense and of course it was the process that had to take place given the circumstances. All I'm thinking about now is how I can do it in here.

Saturday 6th October 2007

I feel so frustrated. Sometimes I wonder why people do the jobs that they do. Sometimes certain members of staff come across like they hate even being here. There are some awesome nurses here, really kind, but then there's some who I just wonder why they are here. Ironic, really, seeing as we are always asked the same thing.

It was my first time having the sausage casserole on full portions instead of introductory portions, which meant there were four sausages and it was a lot bigger than the introductory portion.

You have to eat it within an hour or else it gets taken away and you have to have two Fortisips. I ran out of time and I refused the supplements as I'd already eaten a lot of the meal and the Fortisips just make you feel plain awful. They are beyond filling and just make you bloat. All of a sudden, the nurse on my table turns to me and says, "Well, we need to review your treatment to see why you're actually here." And then in a really sarcastic tone, "Why did you choose it? When you do the menu, you need to choose meals that you can manage." I felt upset and taken aback, but now I'm annoyed because it was the first time I'd had it on full portions, so I didn't know and I still made a good attempt at it. Where's the encouragement?

I've just had enough now, and I feel like I want to give up. I want to feel major hunger again, I want to feel weak, I want to make myself sick to the absolute extremes until I can't do it anymore and my body screams. How messed up does that sound? I know it does, but I hate not doing and feeling those things and feeling how I feel instead.

I just want to hide away and disappear right now.

23:00 pm - I've just done a load of sit ups and cut all my legs. I just feel so frustrated and out of control in my head. The not eating and making myself sick – the feelings I got from it – the release. It's like I've got all the NOT doing it building up inside me, fit to burst, and I don't know what to do with any of it. To be honest I'm completely overwhelmed by it all and I don't even know how to feel.

Friday 12th October 2007

Tonight was an interesting insight into the night staff that we all moan about (because they mostly haven't got a clue). The one on tonight, who was the only staff member in the lounge area after dinner, was a guy who when he started his shift, clearly didn't know it was an eating disorder unit because I heard the nurses tell him! He was sat on the sofa falling asleep, I must have watched his head go at least five times! Why are these people allowed to work in a unit like this??

Saturday 13th October 2007

I am quite late to bed tonight after having a really long chat with one of the nurses. I normally find her quite intimidating, but it was great! Twice tonight, she has approached me and talked to me without me going to her, which I find really hard.

I've been really struggling with thoughts that I'm so much fatter than everyone else, that I shouldn't be in here compared to all the other girls and it just keeps going around and around my head on replay.

She said to me that if making myself sick was just a habit, then by now the urge to do it would be less, but it's not - and that's because there must be a reason that I'm holding on to it, and that I'm getting something out of it, which I guess makes sense and must be true. I don't know what it is but it's something I need to think about. She told me that restricting and making yourself sick as a combination is the most dangerous form of anorexia and that actually, regardless of what I think my BMI is compared to everyone else's here, I need to be here as much as all of the others.

It felt different coming from her – like she was actually talking to ME and that she meant it.

Maybe I need to accept that I am ill, I am in hospital, having to eat food, be watched and have help because it's got to the point where I am not capable of meeting my own needs.

She also said to me, "It sounds like you think you're only here because of the problem with making yourself sick a lot," which is totally true! So I said yes, and she said that isn't right and that I'm seriously underweight.

It's really made me think. She was so lovely and spoke to me, not my eating disorder. It made me feel like maybe she's not lying about my weight because she was so nice and on point about the rest of the things. I'm really glad I spoke to her tonight. I feel better going to sleep for a change.

This diary entry speaks volumes. That one conversation made such a difference in my mood that night. I was suffering with terrible anxiety; constant butterflies in the pit of my stomach, and my thoughts were literally torturing me. It was difficult for me to approach staff (unlike some of the other girls who seemed to do it so easily). I don't know if this made me seem hostile or that I was ok, but I wasn't. It was just that, for me, this part of the treatment was almost as hard as the food itself. As my school reports say, 'Katie must ask for help when she needs it.'

That night, this nurse must have sensed this and took the time to approach me. Not only that, but she spoke to *me*… not the anorexia. This is so important. I think this is why the chat had such an impact. It was real. She honed in on what was actually going on for me and took the time to explain it in a professional way.

In the treatment of anorexia, this is vital. There needs to be a professionalism, but also a sense of talking to the actual person, not the illness. We may all say the same sorts of things – because that's the anorexia talking – but that doesn't mean that we're all the same. *We* are still in there - we just need someone to help bring out our rational thinking. The same old cliché phrases get frustrating. It feels so textbook, like the same stock response will resonate with all of us because we're all just anorexic.

Don't guilt trip. Don't question whether we really want to get well or say that we need to evaluate our treatment plan because we can't finish a meal. No. Good, old-fashioned, honest conversations to uncover the real, underlying issues is what's needed. This is how help should be.

How patients are spoken to has the power to make or break treatment. We need hope. We need rational explanation. If only for a moment, that conversation gave me those things. And these moments are critical to the recovery process. The picture has to build slowly. When someone first goes in to hospital, their brain is starved and they will be irrational. Nothing you say will help or make a difference. They are physically and mentally malnourished, and at this point they just need kind hearts and patience.

Once someone starts eating again, they can begin to think about the reasons behind their eating disorder. It's at this point that it's so important to have a meaningful conversation. Everyone will be different in how long it takes for them to start putting pieces of the puzzle together, and then to accept them and work with them. If someone doesn't figure out the reasons and patterns behind their behaviour, then they will never be willing to let it go. They will just return to the unbearable thoughts and feelings. If they know the reasons behind why they feel this way, there is hope that it can change and that there might - just might - be a way out.

Monday 15th October 2007

I'm obsessed with thinking that I'm so much fatter than everyone else, that I don't deserve treatment, that I came in too early.

I asked the dietician today what my BMI was, and when she told me what it was, and I freaked. She was lovely (this is a nice dietician, not the horrible one from before) and tried to show me on her chart where BMI's are in categories of 'underweight', 'severely underweight', 'death possible' and 'death imminent.' I am in the 'death possible' category... you would think that maybe this would help me see things clearly, but instead, I have spent the whole day going over and over and over in my head how I should have refused admission. I should have pushed it another month. If I'd had pushed it that bit further, maybe I would have felt better about treatment and gaining weight. That I didn't push it it's full course, I didn't complete what needs to be done, I didn't get to the bottom, the end - I didn't die.

The dietician said that one of the reasons eating disorders are scary is because although you may feel ok, it is not possible at this weight for your insides to be working properly and sometimes there are no warning signs – your body just gives in and stops working.

I spoke to another patient who told me that they also feel this exact way about the same thing, so that made me feel a little better. I tried to explain it to one of the nurses in my ward about how this was really gnawing at my brain, and he basically said that we, "Needed to steer away from this topic" and that I need to "move on." I was absolutely gutted as I'd finally found the courage to say it, which was really hard as I feel so messed up for thinking it, and then that is what I get told... How do I just move on when it's all I can think? It's literally tearing me apart inside. My brain feels like a record stuck on repeat. Do they not think that if it's annoying them, then it must be completely driving me insane?

WALK THROUGH DARKNESS

Friday 19th October 2007

I decided to write down how I've been feeling about this 'not being thin enough' obsession and take it to my occupational therapy appointment. This was really hard after the last response I got, but I know how lovely the occupational therapist is and so she seemed like a good person to speak about it with.

It was a FAB conversation! It's really got me thinking! It was like a little light switch went on somewhere, and so I am going to try and make some sense of it so I can look back at this tomorrow.

We were talking about why I feel the need to hit the very bottom. Why is being the thinnest in here so important to me? Why don't I want anyone to be better at it than me? She asked me whether there was anything else in my life that made me feel the need to be the best or I will have failed. Was this a pattern? I told her that this pretty much applies to everything I've ever done.

I told her about my love for drama and how my dad had not approved. And that I was crushed when I didn't hear back from the Doctor's audition. When I left college, I never did drama again because in my mind, I had failed and I couldn't bear it.

I told her that in all of my sales jobs, I had been the top seller but I put so much pressure on myself to be the best that it burned me out. I also felt that everyone else expected me to be the best. And when the pressure got too much, I left and moved on to another job.

I told her how I felt that everything I'd ever done could have been 'a little bit better.' Even things like when I went to visit my dad, I used to get anxious and upset on the way home because I was wracked with thoughts that maybe I didn't stay long enough, maybe I didn't say the right things, maybe I wasn't a good enough daughter. Then there's my relationships. I just feel like I've never been content or happy with my life. There has always been this hole. It started when I was around 15, when the depression kicked in and I started self-harming.

I told her that I'm afraid of never feeling happy or content with anything. This eating disorder is the same thing, just in a different context. It's another 'all or nothing' situation that I've put myself in. It's a private thing – it's my thing. It's something that I can do, that I can do well, that I can complete right down to the very last step - that very last 'category' on that stupid BMI chart... 'death imminent.'

132

Weight loss is very regimented. It's measured by numbers, BMI's, how unwell you feel and how thin you look. You can track your progress easily, you can track how 'good' you are at it. You can find charts to compare your age, height and weight with others. You can even see how far the textbook says you are from dying. To me, that was just the last 'notch' to reach to prove to myself that I did it. That's why I hated it when people said, "You came just in time." It meant that I DIDN'T do it.

That's why this comparing myself to others is such a big issue for me. I feel gutted, just like I did all of those other times in my life that I haven't done things I set out to do, or that people have done better than me.

And that's it. That's my conclusion. That's what this has been – I wanted to be as thin as possible, eat as little as possible, throw up as much as possible, push myself as much as possible, be as close to death as I possibly could without actually dying – or if it came to that, then so be it. I wanted to reach that very end point to prove to myself that I'd done it, completed it, done it the best I possibly could.

But also to block out everything I've been feeling – the pressure to do something with my life... not feeling good enough, guilt, debts... Having a 'goal' helped to block out other feelings. Obsessing about this meant that I wasn't thinking about everything else as much – it was just weight, BMI numbers, calories and feeling ill, which was all good because it reminded me of my progress.

I'm not saying that I've figured it all out and that it's all going to be fine from now on. Because it's not. I also have been thinking over the last however many days that in this process, I've actually given myself a million more problems. So now I have those to contend with on top of the problems I already had. So, I don't know where this is going to end or how I'm possibly going to get through it all, but at least maybe something's come together a little? Maybe I'll look back on this tomorrow and think it doesn't make much sense - nothing else I think seems to make much sense. But for now, I think it does and that's all that matters.

Now I feel really confused though, because I still don't want to gain weight and I'm still so scared. I'm not sure where I'm supposed to go from here?

How do you let go of something you want to keep? Even if it's bad?

Something that makes you happy but keeps you feeling sad,

You want to let it go, but keep it close inside,

You want to feel free – but you also want to hide,

Behind that wall you've built that keeps you feeling strong,

It's the one thing that's worked, feels right, yet also feels so wrong,

It pushes you and pushes you to just reach that goal,

To reach that one moment when you finally feel whole,

To fill that gap you've felt through everything you've done,

With this you just keep going – to finally feel you've won,

To know you've reached the point where you can do no more,

To finally realise what it's all been for,

To reach that absolute limit would mean you have achieved,

But in reality, when you get there could you really just leave?

Just stop, walk away and believe it was enough?

Or would there be another goal to make it that bit more tough?

To push that little more to test that the 'end' was indeed the 'end'

And all those rules you'd made would they really now just bend?

Would hovering on life and death really close the chapter?

Would it really make you feel like you'd got what you were after?

How would you know that the 'end' was really here?

Would you finally feel thin? Feel ill? Be filled with sudden fear?

Or could the "end" always just be pushed a little more?

Until only real death would make you completely sure?

Without knowing it, I had had a 'lightbulb moment.'

At the time, I don't think I realised how important this realisation was. I was too caught up in the idea of weight – scared to death of putting it back on. In the days leading up to this, the conversations I'd had with some of the staff on the unit had clearly got me thinking. Something had resonated, and this was a significant moment.

My problem, in its essence, was perfectionism.

People often talk about perfectionism rather flippantly, saying things like, "I'm a perfectionist because I like things to be tidy." I'm talking about true perfectionism. Aiming for the unobtainable. Aiming for flawlessness. Aiming for unachievable goals. The type of perfectionism that interferes with all your life and its functioning. People gripped by perfectionism are constantly aiming for success. But what we're actually doing is avoiding failure. So we're aiming for success, but with a negative drive. This is toxic from the get-go.

It's a constantly critical inner voice. I would go as far as to say that everyone I've ever met with anorexia has also been in the grip of perfectionism. It's almost like the two go hand-in-hand.

Of course, everyone's reason for having an eating disorder is different. However, perfectionism seems to be a common driving force. Add an inner-perfectionist to a deadly anorexic voice and you have a confused, frustrated and potentially, very ill person. My brain felt like it was tied in knots; twisted, pushed and pulled from every single direction. It's a terrible way of being.

Before you can begin to let those anorexic behaviours go, you have to find what's behind that voice. What the real fears are. This isn't instantaneous. I'm *still* learning. But the lightbulb moments are good - they are *so* good. Even if you don't realise it at the time.

I will never forget one of my cognitive behavioural therapy (CBT) groups with the wonderful psychiatrist who ran the eating disorder unit. He did a visual explanation with two tennis balls, four ping pong balls and some marbles. First, he put the marbles in a jar, then the ping pong balls and then the tennis balls. But the lid wouldn't go on. We then had to figure out how to get them all into the jar and get the lid to close. If you do it the other way around, so the tennis balls go in first and then the ping pong balls, then the marbles could fit in the cracks and the lid closes.

He looked at us all and said, "Imagine that this is your brain. If you focus on all the little things first (the marbles), then by the time you get to the big things (the tennis balls), there is no room left for you to think about them. Whereas, if you sort the big things out first, all the little things will just slot into place."

This particular psychiatrist is one of the most amazing people I've ever met within the mental health services. He made sense. He was honest. He was what every psychiatrist should aim to be. Of course, at the time no one liked him because he was the unit's driving force. By that point, I'd had many difficult experiences with professionals – and I was to have many more – but there are diamonds out there. They can be hard to find. I was lucky enough to have found my diamond doctor.

I was going through a period of reflection. I was trying desperately to cling on to the things that I'd realised and the things that had resonated with me. I understood that no goal was ever going to be enough; I had thought that one weight would mean 'I've done it'; then a little less; then 80 pounds; then when I was told that I needed to be an inpatient - surely there was nothing else I would be able to do? But then I was tortured by the fact that I didn't get to that very last category on that BMI chart: death imminent. It would never have been enough. What's more, you don't always get the 'death imminent' warning. My heart could have just given out and that would have been it. No second chances. No euphoria of hitting that 'ultimate goal.' Just death.

Finally, I realised that even if I had lost a bit more weight - even If I had refused admission and carried on with my endless quest - I would have had to go into hospital anyway. It would have been voluntary, or I would have been sectioned (or I would have carried on until I died). Nothing would have been any different. Going from 6 stone to 7 stone would have been exactly the same as if I'd gone in at 5 stone and got up to 6 stone. The feelings would have been the same. The process was inevitable – awful and inevitable. In my mind, I realised that the treatment process had to start somewhere or I would have died. There was no middle ground. Realising this gave me comfort. It was something that I took with me long after my recovery. For some people with anorexia, this may not resonate, but for me knowing that it was inevitable made me feel like something had been lifted from my shoulders slightly.

However, this did not mean that it all magically went away. I was still fighting the demons and battling the thoughts. Gaining more and more weight was hard to deal with. New patients arriving was a terrible trigger for those familiar thoughts that I was so much bigger than everyone else and that I didn't deserve treatment. Each day brought a new challenge, a new trigger, something else that set me back and left me trying to cling to these little rays of hope.

Wednesday 24th October 2007

I've refused lots of meals. I'm getting so big and my brain is constantly spinning. In the ward rounds, I was told they were discussing sectioning me! But because my BMI is 15, he said he doesn't have the grounds to section me. I've been offered a 'break from treatment' for a week if I want it, to think about what I really want. I may take it. I feel like I need time away from here.

I'm also getting put on some medication. He said that because my anorexic thoughts are so strong, it seems impossible for me to do anything but listen to it, whereas this will apparently make it possible to swing back to the middle. This is fine by me. In fact, I welcome it because the thoughts I'm having all day, every day are driving me mad. I literally can't think. I can't think over my brain, which is constantly turning and churning and thinking and analysing - it just won't stop. So I really don't mind, apart from the fact that he told me not to be shocked if I read the leaflet as it's also used in treatment for people with schizophrenia and psychosis... I'm not sure why I would need something like that, but if it helps, I guess I will try it.

Thursday 25th October 2007

I've decided to take the week's 'break from treatment.' Being around so many people with the same problem is making it too hard for me to think straight. I desperately want some home comforts and some space to myself. I don't know whether I will go and eat as I should. Of course, that's what I plan, but then that voice is screaming that it's also an opportunity to restrict massively. I just need out for a bit. I feel like maybe something has changed slightly in my head, but it's hard to hear it over this constant screaming in my brain and constant looking around me and hearing other people's conversations about things that my brain is already screaming isn't helping me at this point.

In eating disorder treatment, you usually start from a point of absolute denial – total unwillingness to get well or to make any kind of change. But I think there comes a point in most people's treatment where you drive up to a crossroads. You see two paths. One is brightly lit and you can see familiar obstacles. You've gone down this path before and though there are many obstacles, they have become part of your nature and you know what you're dealing with. But at the end of that path, there is a dark, steep cliff and if you hover too near to the edge, you will plummet. But you are confident that you know what you are doing and that you will not fall off the edge. That sort of thing only happens in movies, right?

The other path is totally black. You can't see anything, you don't know what's down there. You would essentially be stumbling blind. But at the end of that path, there is a light and it looks inviting. It's a long path. It seems so desperately far away, and first, you have to walk through the darkness. That absolutely terrifying darkness.

Which would you choose?

DEAR ANOREXIA

I arrived home and immediately felt guilty. They were right: this should be fantastic; the flat should be fantastic; and the prospect of university should be fantastic. Why didn't I feel fantastic? Why did I just feel dread and utter confusion?

I was supposed to be 'recovered.' I was a healthy weight. I had a new home. Everyone thought this was it. I was 'over it.' Well, that's what I thought they were thinking. People had stopped looking at me in the way that they did when I was thin. That was an illness that people could see – it was tangible. But now? Now I thought that I should be better, because I believed that's how people saw me. I couldn't process it and I didn't know how to move forward.

For weeks I had been thinking that I would come out and just lose a bit of weight. Maybe then I would feel more comfortable in my own skin – more ready to conquer what lay ahead? I didn't feel confident. I had put on more weight than what I thought my recovered self should look like. I just needed to feel comfortable with myself and then I could enjoy my supposedly fantastic life.

Friday 15th February 2008

This isn't going too well. I've been trying to eat, but I've made myself sick. I can't do this! Rob says I have to and that I have no choice, but he doesn't understand, no one does, which makes this so frustrating.

I went to the doctor's today to get my olanzapine and he said, 'well you've obviously put on a bit of weight since the last time I saw you.' Fucking great. That's just about the single most awful thing someone could say to me at this moment in time.

I'm so lost. I don't fit into an anorexic brain, nor my own brain, nor either body, and I feel like I'm hovering somewhere above, just looking and watching.

Friday 22nd February 2008

Things are not going well. The doctor said that if I carry on losing weight so quickly I will have to go back into hospital. Everyone is saying that I've lost loads really quickly, but I can't see it, it feels like nothing and I feel it's been coming off slowly. I just want this weight off of me!

All I've eaten the last three days is three rich tea biscuits a day, any more than that I just can't allow myself; I make myself sick. I was told by the psychologist that she's going to have to have a word with the team because I won't be able to survive very long on what I'm eating. I just can't stop myself; it's not that I don't want to eat. I do! I'm hungry and I even miss the hospital food! Who ever thought I'd be saying that?! But I feel too guilty, too fat, and too disgusting when I do, and that just overrides everything.

Things with me and Rob weren't as beautiful as I thought they'd be once I was out. We weren't doing anything together. He was constantly going out. I'd make an effort to eat dinner together, only for him to announce that once again he was 'off out.' I tried to eat and tried to stick to something that resembled a routine, but it always ended with my head down the toilet.

In my diary entries I talk about it like a drug addict getting their fix. My safe place was the bathroom. I felt the anxiety and tension slip away as I pushed my body to the limit once again with the amount that I was making myself sick. It was almost a form of self-harm. As well as a weight-loss tactic, I was pushing my body to the extreme, almost wanting to feel the pain it caused.

Within three weeks of leaving the hospital, I had lost a significant amount of weight, but t didn't feel like it was enough. Before I knew it, I was trapped, once again, in the grips of that anorexic voice in my head. This time it was even more viscous, because look at all the weight I'd lost before, how well I was doing then, and look at me now. It seemed like I was never going to feel comfortable in the clothes or my body. I'd put all this disgusting weight back on and now I was stuck with it. It was all my own doing. I ate the food. I had the misplaced hope. And now look at me.

I realised that it wasn't about looking thin. Actually, when I came out of hospital and lost an initial few pounds, I was okay with how I looked physically. It was the numbers. I was obsessed with the goddamn numbers and the success that I attached to those numbers. I had a certain number in my mind. As long as I was below that number, everything felt safe. If I went over that number, however, things felt out of control.

I have always struggled with OCD to some extent. When I was younger and living with my mum I had to kiss my teddies (there were a lot of them) in order, one by one, every night. If I felt that I hadn't done it properly, or, God forbid, I missed one out, I had to go back and start the whole procedure again. The need to 'check' and to know where things are has followed me through my life. I have learned to control it over the years and what was once a daily check is now once a week I guess this would stem somewhere from my childhood. There also seems to be an obsessive nature running through my mum's side of the family.

At that point in my life, however, the obsession took over. I would walk around in a blind panic, checking the same things over and over and over again. I'd get back to the start, wonder if I had indeed just gone through that 20-minute process, and then start it all over again. I would cry and scream through pure frustration. I would be go around in circles for hours at a time.

It then took over my sleep. I'd be up late checking everything over and over to satisfy the anxiety in my head to fall asleep. Then, when I finally did fall asleep, from pure exhaustion, I would wake up numerous times in the night and the first thing I would think about was checking. I would be doing all of it again in the middle of the night.

I remember sitting on the end of my bed one night, with my head in my hands, sobbing. It was that loud explosive sobbing that happens when you feel completely broken. The anorexic voice was screaming at me. The OCD was violently poking around in my head. They were a toxic combination that made me cling to the feeling of control even tighter.

Towards the end of March 2008, just shy of six-weeks from being discharged, I had lost a significant amount of weight.. Looking back, of course I can see how quick that weight loss was, but at the time I didn't see it. It seemed so slow. I felt like I had to have it off my body immediately.

At the time, I also found out that my mum had been diagnosed with a brain tumor. She had been getting terrible headaches. But still, it seemed to come from nowhere. I don't think she told me the full extent of the problems she had been having prior to the diagnosis. I was devastated and so worried that she was going to die. She had been told that it was a meningioma, which meant that there was a 95% chance that it was benign, but all I saw was that 5% chance that it wasn't, and that she was going to be taken away from me.

I was living on three rich tea biscuits a day. That was it. That was all that I would allow myself. Anything more and I threw it up. Again, this didn't mean that I didn't crave food. The body naturally does. Regardless of what my brain was doing, my body was screaming out for food and being around it was torture. Sometimes it took all of my energy not to stare at someone while they were eating, imagining what it tasted like. That's how strong that anorexic voice is. It can squash even nature's powerful cries for food. Anorexia screams louder than anything else. It's a piercing shrill that you can't ignore.

Saturday 22nd March 2008

I'm eating less than before I went into hospital and I didn't think that was possible. I've started to wonder whether my body is going to be able to keep going on what I'm having …

Today while I was at my nan's house there was so much food ... Chippy pies, plates of sausage egg and beans … I would have done anything for that fucking sausage egg and beans. But I had to sit there chewing my chewing gum with the voice in my head screaming, 'no, you don't want to ruin it now, look at all the work you've put in. It'll taste nice for a really short time and then think about how you're going to feel after.' Mum was trying to get me to just have one piece of bread with two chips on it. I couldn't even do that.

Both my mind and my behaviour were totally out of control. One day, I ate some sweets and then spent 50 minutes in the bathroom. I don't know how I didn't give myself a heart attack. My hair was lank and thin and falling out. I was permanently freezing cold. I was getting chest pains and living on nothing, yet I was still trying to figure out ways to dodge doctors' appointments so that I could make it to at least my previous admission weight, preferably a bit less, before they sent me back to hospital. I knew it was coming, but I was in the grips of anorexia more than ever before. My brain was being suffocated by it. I couldn't bear the thought of not being allowed to get this weight off me before they tried to take it away again.

One day, I was looking back on my diary entries, trying to find a time of relative positivity. I knew that my outlook had been very different not long before, and I wanted to see if I could gain any insight from it. That's when I realised how quickly I'd lost the weight. I saw that it had taken me almost 5 months to lose the weight before going into hospital the previous time. Yet here I was, two months after leaving the hospital and nearly at my original admission weight. It had felt like so much more than two months, but it wasn't. That was all it took to fall more dangerously and helplessly into anorexia's arms than ever before.

I was totally food obsessed. I would look at pictures online. I would pour over menus that I would never order from. I would fall asleep at night – after my checking procedures – thinking about McDonalds, KFC and Pizza hut. I dreamed about food and woke up in a panic thinking that I'd eaten it. It would take me awhile to realise that it was only a dream and I didn't need to head to bathroom. Nonetheless, I convinced myself though that I was okay. I just needed to get to yet another certain weight and my brain would be free for good.

Friday 11th April 2008

I somehow feel like I have never experienced anorexia up until now, it's in a whole new league this time that I never even thought existed. The thoughts seem so much stronger, the actual fear of food is so much bigger and the preoccupation seems so much worse. As for the physical side of things I wonder what I was even complaining about before ... I feel like I can't breathe and I'm so cold I've got a sleeping bag on the bed on top of the duvet.

The psychologist has told me to prepare myself for my appointment with the doctor on the 29th to be told that I need to go back into hospital and to be prepared for it to be quicker because I'm eating so little and my behaviour is worse. So now I'm terrified in case they section me.

I'm scared that even if I do go in that this time I won't be able to eat and that I will be sectioned and end up with a tube. I don't want that, but this is so strong this time I don't know whether I can beat it.

I carried on desperately trying to lose what I could as quickly as I could before the doctors could get to me. I really felt that I needed to get to less than my previous admission date for the anorexia to quieten down. If they got there first that was never going to happen.

I had lost a lot of weight in 10 weeks. Looking back, I'm surprised that I didn't end up in a hospital because of my general health; losing that amount of weight in that short amount of time would have put tremendous stress on my body. Of course I didn't see it. Even when I had the flu and my blood sugar level dropped and I started shaking uncontrollably and I dropped to the floor heaving and heaving. I allowed myself a cup of tea with sugar and one piece of toast. Nothing more. Even then I was more concerned about the fact that I had just had all that sugar and toast than the fact that I could have passed out on my own and been in real trouble.

For me I wasn't losing quickly enough. It was painfully slow. I had gone 10 weeks on nothing more than the three rich tea biscuits a day. I was pushing my body to the absolute limit and I was extremely lucky that it didn't give up on me. I couldn't even cry. I didn't even have tears to spare. I was a total shell just wandering around in a daze.

The week leading up to my doctor's appointment the psychologist told me to prepare to go back to hospital the following week. I didn't care about anything. She asked me what I thought would happen if I didn't go back into hospital. I simply looked at her and said that I would carry on and that I would die. She told me that my body was in the starvation stage and expressed concerns that, 'I was talking about dying with about as much emotion as talking about the carpet.' She also said that she wondered with me

153

sometimes whether what I was doing was a way to become invisible. It was a way to cut myself off from everything, to protect myself and so I could almost pretend like I wasn't there. And whether giving it up and going back into hospital were so scary because it was like saying 'I'm here.' She pretty much nailed it.

On 6th April 2008, I was readmitted. I'd done what I had been aiming for: I was lower than my previous admission weight. But of course, it wasn't enough and the usual thoughts plagued me once again.

The dietician was shocked when I told her what I'd eaten for 10 weeks. She said she'd never heard anything like it and that I was lucky to still be alive. One of the nurses who had known me previously told me that 'I looked like crap.' I took some satisfaction from that, understanding that by crap she meant thin. Everyone told me how much worse I looked this admission. I couldn't see it. Although I had hit my target the anorexia was screaming that I could have done more.

There was no way to win ... I was a failure for not losing enough weight, or I was a failure for not doing recovery well enough. I was a failure for letting all the nurses on the unit down. I was paranoid that they thought I was a pathetic attention seeker. Back on the olanzapine I went.

I was given a task of writing two letters to anorexia the friend, and anorexia the enemy.

Anorexia the friend

Dear Anorexia,

In some strange way I am grateful for you coming in to my life. For years I had felt unhappy, depressed and suicidal at times, but when you came along you helped to change that, you gave me focus, something to aim for – a purpose I suppose.

You numbed everything and stopped me from thinking about anything else. All that mattered was you. As long as those numbers on the scales went down then everything was ok and the sense of achievement I got from those numbers was fantastic. I was finally good at something and it seemed like nothing could match that.

I liked looking in the mirror and seeing bones and my clothes not fitting me, people tell me that it's horrible but to me it showed that I was doing well and getting where I needed to be. The same goes for feeling ill – as much as I hated it and it scared me, I also like it because again it proved to you that I was pushing myself as much as I could and as long as I was pushing myself then I could feel content with myself. Ultimately this is what I am scared of losing.

You also acted as an excuse for me. With you, at my worst, I couldn't do anything and if I couldn't do anything then I couldn't fail at anything and if I couldn't fail at anything then I couldn't let myself of anyone else down. You relieved me of the expectations that I feel there are from myself and other people.

You helped me to feel happier with my body, as long as I could see those bones and feel the clothes hanging off me, I'd know that physically I wasn't fat. When I ate nothing and felt that hunger I was happy in the knowledge that I was empty with nothing to weigh me down or make me gain weight.I enjoyed that emptiness, the floatiness and the fuzziness it gave me. The artificial high of being completely in control.

I am scared to let you go. To watch the bones disappear, feel my clothes becoming tighter again, feeling a failure and losing that control.

The truth is that I don't know what to be without you, part of me wished that you could just stay in my life.

Anorexia the enemy

Dear Anorexia,

I wish more than anything that you had never come into my life. You have made me so confused and unhappy and completely stolen the last two-years of my life. All my life has been for the last two years is calories, weight, numbers and counting … constantly counting!

You have made me scared of food to the point that I won't even chew gum anymore. And I love food! Because of you I am now terrified of it, even when I have felt so ill and unbelievably tired you have made me feel so guilty for having so much as a cup of tea.

You made me a slave to the scales. A maintenance in weight or a gain so much as half a pound made me feel like a total failure and changed my mood and outlook for the rest of that day.

You have ruined my relationship because ALL I could think about is you. I have driven Rob to the point of despair, constantly asking him questions about whether I look fat and whether I've gained weight. When he answers me I still can't rest because you make me believe that he, and everyone else, is lying or they just don't see the truth.

I haven't been able to go for meals, go to the cinema, go for a drink or anything else that involves consuming any calories, even though I'd love to. I feel like I've done nothing but be in hospital – first day-care then inpatient and now inpatient again, by the time I've finished this stay I will have probably wasted about a year of my life. At 22 years old, that's a year that I should be enjoying. Instead, the last two-years have been a blur and I have nothing to show for them.

You always make me feel that no matter what I do it's never good enough. The weight is never low enough. I'm not ill enough to get help. And there's always another goal to reach that will apparently make me feel better, but it never does it just carries on going.

I feel so confused that I don't know what to think. I HATE you and I wish more than anything that I could just make you disappear.

Once again, I was stuck at a crossroad, realising that neither of the available paths had actually helped me. I was left wondering where the hell I was supposed to go from here. I was drained. I felt like I had no fight left in me. Deep down, I knew that I needed to dig deep to find some strength to begin to fight again. I just didn't know if there was any point. I had been there, done that, and bought the t-shirt. Where had it got me? Exactly where I started. I was in a vicious cycle that I couldn't see any way out of. I started to believe that this was going to be my life. I was never going to be able to live without this voice and without this attitude to food. I just didn't see how anything that I did was going to make any of it better in the long term. That was soul destroying.

HOPE THROUGH FEAR

Friday 26th October 2007

Well, I'm still here. Not through choice.

I decided to take the time out. I told Rob and he came, he sat down and simply said, "Well, there's a bit of a snag to that." To cut a long story short, he lost his job. He applied for, and was told that he had got, a security job but they have told him now that he hasn't... so he couldn't pay the rent and he already handed the keys back on Tuesday, and all of our stuff is at his nan's house.

So now I have no home. Even if I wanted to leave here, I can't because I have nowhere to go and I feel so backed into a corner. I feel like I've messed up both our lives. It is surely my fault that this has happened. If I was well and working, then none of this would have even happened.

I just can't believe it. Why does it seem like my life just goes from one disaster to the next?

I loved that flat. It was my home. Now I don't have anywhere to call my own. Nowhere to call home.

Sunday 28th October 2007

I keep thinking that I want to go home... then I realise that I have no home to go to.

I'm trying to cling to those rational thoughts. I know I'm here because I've starved myself. I was spending God knows how much time with my head down the toilet, most of the time hating every second of it despite the relief from the voice inside my head. Eating so much as a rice cake and feeling like the world was going to end. Feeling so angry and out of control... do I really want to go back to that?

I'm really not a fan of this medication. It totally zonks me out and I feel sick with it, but on the other hand, I feel like I am starting to see the other side whereas before there wasn't one. I look at all the other patients in here and see how thin they are, the preoccupation, the tormented minds and I realise that's me, too. I am probably being looked at in the same way and I don't want to be that person... well, PART of me wants to be that person, but deep down I think I'm just scared of changing. I'm scared the weight gain will make it seem like I'm fine when I'm not. I'm scared of what will happen. I'm even scared of day to day life. I'm scared I won't become anything, I'll go back to jobs I don't like, that I will never feel happy or content with anything. I'm scared of myself.

Wednesday 31st October

I feel totally deflated at the moment. I've woken up feeling like the rug has been pulled from underneath my feet. I think I've realised that I have no choice in this. I have to let it go. I am going to put on weight, and there's no use in trying to fight it.

The thoughts have subsided a bit. They are still there but it's not screaming like before. Maybe it's the medication. I'm not sure, but it's a bit quieter. Instead, though, I've been left with this horrible feeling of flatness. It's strange, I almost feel uneasy not having the screaming on repeat in my head which is completely backwards, I know, seeing as how it was making me feel.

It's a similar feeling to when I've given up other things or not felt good enough, like I've given something else up - just given in.

I've eaten everything that's been put in front of me and I haven't really spoken to anyone because I just feel like, what's the point? The same conversations, same answers, still heading in the same direction. It seems pointless.

I have had moments, recently, where despite having no home, I've felt more positive. It's like part of me has accepted this, which has made things a bit easier but also left me feeling a sense of defeat and hopelessness. So once again, I'm left feeling confused and unsure about what to think.

I just wish I could go home and everyone would leave me alone.

I got leave on Saturday 2pm-5pm, and apparently a social worker is coming to see me at some point to discuss housing and how I can get help with that. It all just feels like so much. Sometimes I look forward to bedtime, just so that I can be on my own.

In the following weeks, I was battling a feeling of flatness. It was almost grief; the feeling that I'd lost something really important to me. I spent a lot of time clinging on to the rays of rationality that I had found. I was still battling the powerful anorexic voice and a lot of depressive feelings, but I was also feeling calmer, a little more focused and less caught up in it all. It was as if the new medication had freed up some space in my mind; it allowed some of my actual thoughts to seep through... very slowly, but it was a start.

It's quite a disorienting stage. I felt like I wanted to get well, but at the same time, I hated it. And I was more aware of all the feelings because I wasn't numb from starvation anymore.

I became very aware of people's behaviour. I was upset that my step mum hadn't contacted me in six weeks. I knew that she and dad had split up, and our relationship hadn't been plain sailing, but I had lived with her as my family for all those years.

Then other people unexpectedly came to the forefront, which confused me. My Brother, for example. I had grown up with him when living with my mum. I had adored him. I loved him very much. I looked up to him and I remember always feeling just that little bit safer at school, knowing that I had a big brother that I could call on. I have a vivid memory of being sat under the duvet with him on Christmas morning, singing, "Why are we waiting? We are suffocating." (Which in itself holds a lot of irony!) I look back and think how utterly awful it must have been for him when one day I was just gone, without any real explanation. One moment, we were a part of each other's everyday life, and the next, it was like we didn't exist to each other.

I met up with him a couple of times soon after leaving my mum's house. One time we went on a trip to the swimming baths. He tried to ask me why I had left and told me how bad things were. I tried to ignore it. The truth was that I had no words. I had no real explanation. Deep down, I was confused myself. I just wanted to pretend that none of it had ever happened at all. I tried to compartmentalise what was going on, even at that young age – to just exist for the moment. I can still revert to this way of thinking and behaving. I have been told by many a doctor and therapist that it's almost disturbing how I can speak of some horrific events as if I am recounting the weather. I almost detach myself completely from the situation and feelings. When I look back at some things from my childhood, I get upset for that little girl, without connecting her to me.

Over time, we just lost contact. I missed him terribly. He did try and make contact when he was a bit older, but by this point coupled with what was going on within me emotionally, I felt uncomfortable. Like there was an elephant in the room that I felt I had created and was trying to pretend wasn't there. I no longer felt like I had the same connection with him. But I wanted it so badly that any contact always ended with tears, frustration and just generally feeling shitty about myself. I felt like the whole goddamn thing was just my fault, and I was a terrible person.

When he came to visit me in hospital, I was so anxious and uncomfortable. We hadn't had a real relationship in so long, and now he was seeing me massively underweight and broken. I didn't want him to see me like that. I found it unbearable. From his point of view, I'm sure, he was reaching out a hand to his sister whom he had loved – showing that he cared. Because of my own guilt and anxiety, I pushed him away in many ways. I probably came across uninterested and like I just wanted to be left alone. The irony was that I did want to be left alone. I'd had too many people who didn't understand or who were uninterested that I didn't know how to react to those who genuinely did. I was always second guessing whether there was an ulterior motive – why on earth would anyone be interested in me?

Sadly, I later managed to kill any remaining relationship we had. I was going through a good period and starting to take part in beauty pageants. To enter, you needed a sponsor. I had never had any problems finding sponsors, but it occurred to me during one pageant to ask my brother to be my sponsor. I knew that he was doing well, working in high-up positions in bars and clubs, and I was proud. I admired him for doing so well. I wanted him to be a part of something that I was doing. But I think it hit a nerve with him. He saw me as being like everyone else, just trying to get something from him. That couldn't have been further from the truth. I wanted him to be proud of me and what I was doing. But it backfired.

I can understand why he probably thought that, I would have no doubt felt exactly the same. There was miscommunication and individual thoughts and feelings that clashed without either of us realising why. The day I left my mom's, I felt like I had lost a brother in a heartbeat. He was left with the aftermath. I was desperate to get that back but went about it the wrong way.

We are both older and wiser now, with children and families of our own. I hope, as we have recently gotten back in touch, that we can start to rebuild and move forward, as I certainly have missed my big brother.

When I left my mum's house and lost a brother, I gained a new younger brother at my dad's house. I grew to love him very much. Whereas before, I had felt untouchable because I had a big brother to protect me, I now found myself being the protective one. I wanted him to grow up happy and to feel like people cared (I guess the opposite to how I had felt as a child). I loved to feed him, play with him and take care of him.

We used to go to a child minder, who I hated. She was supposed to be looking after us, but I always ended up feeding him, changing his nappies and playing with him. I didn't mind because at least that way I could make sure that he was being looked after properly.

I remember picking him up from school and listening to him tell me about what he had done, and I kept (and still have) some pictures that he did in nursery. I took great pride in teaching him how to tie his shoelaces and later, teaching him how to play chopsticks on the keyboard. I really loved my little brother, and in many ways, it made up for the heartache I felt losing my big brother.

Unfortunately, he grew up troubled. He had his own issues and got into frequent trouble. There were times where everyone turned their backs on him. Some might say that this was understandable, given the trouble he got into. But I never did. He would often come to my house and I would give him his tea, watch films and talk to him. I tried to get him to open up to me. It was very clear to me that he had his own mental health issues and was hurting about a lot of things. But he struggled to open up. I saw a lot of myself in him. He was now the black sheep in the family, the one in all the trouble, and no one knew what to do with him. But I knew that deep down he was a good kid with a good heart. He was just hurting. He had his issues and somewhere along the line he had lost himself. But I always had faith that he would find himself again. He just needed some support, someone that would always be there, no matter what. Someone with no ulterior motive, no hidden agenda - someone that just loved him and wanted to be there for him because they cared. I was that person. Well, I tried to be that person. I never turned him away and always made it clear that I was always there for him.

When he got his own place and had nothing, I bought him towels, cutlery, a kettle and other bits and pieces to try to help. Later, it came out that he was living in a flat infested with mice and illegal immigrants all squashed into the living room. It was filthy, disgusting and totally uninhabitable. It seemed that my dad, who I no longer spoke to, was doing nothing to help. So, I got in touch with a homeless charity that offered shared-accommodation and help with council applications.

The charity told us that the shared accommodation would provide other support too, such as access to education. It sounded like it could really help to get him back on track and I told him that it sounded like the best option – especially because the council application would most likely be a longer process.

At this time, my own mood had turned and I was struggling with depression. It went downhill rapidly. But I made sure that I was still there to help him. I was due to have an assessment at the Priory, but the charity called me to make an appointment as soon as possible to support my brother. So, I pushed back my Priory appointment. My brother asked me if his girlfriend could come. I said no, as they wouldn't house them together. It was a single application and my priority was making sure he was ok.

They offered him something, but he turned it down saying that he wanted his own flat. What broke my heart was that he told me via a Facebook message that I had pushed him to go to the charity and it wasn't what he had wanted. It sounded just like my dad. I was completely taken aback. I had given him my opinion. The supported accommodation would be a better option because of the support – which he didn't have a lot of. What's more, most people in the charity's share accommodation go on to get their own council flat within 12-months. I had in no way forced him in to it.

He was clearly upset that I had said no to his girlfriend coming, and he obviously believed that I was being forceful or trying to tell him what to do. I often wonder who said what to him. He told me that I wasn't his parent and said some nasty things that broke my heart. I told him that I was disgusted by how he had spoken to me and that all I wanted to do was help, which was absolutely, genuinely the case.

A week later, I was admitted to the Priory with another brother having exited my life.

It was a blow that I wasn't expecting, and it made me question so much about the world. Sometimes – even with the best intentions – you still end up being the bad guy.

I hope that one day he realises that I had nothing but love for him, and the desire to be there for him. But sometimes, too much as happened and it's too much to get past.

I have always found it ironic that I started life with a brother, then later gained another brother and two stepsisters, yet I have gone so much of my life with no siblings whatsoever for varying reasons that were no one in particular's fault, simply the outcome of a wonderfully typical, disjointed, broken family.

There were also the hospital visits from my dad. For a few weeks after, it all came out about him and my step mum separating, he didn't come see me, he didn't even ring. Then all of a sudden, he's there with his new girlfriend, being the doting dad.

Rob wasn't very reliable. Half the time he didn't even answer his phone. I found this hard. I didn't know who was there because they wanted to be and who was there because they felt like they had to, or should, be.

As usual my nan visited week in and week out, without motive. She's since told me that she often came out of the hospital and let a bus go by while she sat at the bus stop crying. Once again, she was a constant when I needed it.

My medication was doubled. This was very sedating and difficult to deal with. But it definitely helped the obsessive thinking and I soon went on to freely choose chocolate for my snacks (something I hadn't tasted for nearly 12 months). You don't realise how sweet chocolate is until you've not had it for nearly a year. Anorexic or not, that's one incredible moment for your senses right there!

I started feeling good about wanting to get well. The feelings of wanting to be anorexic began to subside. It was a beautiful feeling when that anorexic voice stopped drowning me out. It felt a calmness that

I hadn't felt for so long. It was an acceptance. I no longer needed to fight with myself; my fight was with the anorexic voice, and now I recognised that those were two different things.

I started to realise that while anorexia had fulfilled something inside of me, it wasn't actually getting me anywhere, and I started to feel more prepared to tackle my problems head on. I was granted day-leave on the weekends. I went out for lunch and chose something to eat based on what I wanted, rather than the calories. I still had the urges to make myself sick, but I didn't.

Around the end of November 2007, after I had been in hospital for about two months, I wrote another poem that reflects this positive change in thinking:

Her mind suddenly clear, the darkness has gone.

She finally sees a way to move on.

She takes a step forward instead of one back,

With optimism and hope that she did once lack,

A voice of strength she can now hear,

There's finally hope through the fear,

Hope to keep living, hope to keep her alive,

Replacing a hope to die, there's hope to survive,

As one pathway closes, someone opens a door,

A life of possibilities and potential happiness she's sure,

Now a voice from herself, not just the disorder,

Starting to fight this and get things in order,

Feelings no longer numbed, all these things she can hear,

The world around her appears again with less fear,

Things that were shadowed now move into light,

And for once in a long time she feels able to fight,

Fight the darkness that's hovered around for so long,

All she has to do now is just stay strong.

I carried on complying with treatment and I continued to be granted leave. My sessions with the occupational therapist were always my favourite – I actually found them more useful than the sessions with the psychologist, who I didn't feel I gelled with very well. As I made more realisations in the occupational therapy sessions, the anorexic voice would scream at me. This made me feel angry and out of control.

In one session, we had been talking about things 'left unsaid.' It was a particularly hard session for me as I kept thinking about the metaphorical rug things are swept under. I realised that I was extremely angry about being shouted at all those years ago when my dad found out about the self-harming, and that my dad had never taken the time to talk to me about it.

I thought back to when I lived at home and all the times that I hid in my room while everyone else was downstairs. The amount of times that I was called unsociable and given a hard time about it. The fact of the matter was, unsociable or not, I did it because I was depressed. Depressed, uncomfortable, and utterly unhappy. Nothing was spoken about. I felt like I had to hide. I didn't know what else to do or who else to be. My step mum and I had a pretty terrible relationship and I was angry at how bad it made me feel all those years. I was angry that my dad had always taken her side. I didn't feel sociable or like I wanted to spend time with them, I was extremely confused and very lonely. In my mind, I was the black sheep of the family; I had just wandered in too late and I had no real place.

This brought up mixed feelings. Negative feelings about weight gain would inevitably come up and I'd fight them back down. These are the peaks and troughs of recovery. It's a hard road, dealing with those underlying issues; all the anger and hurt that you have suppressed through controlling your food intake. Sometimes it feels easier to revert to that suppression than to have to deal with the hurt. But, ultimately, dealing with the hurt is absolutely necessary.

By early December, I desperately wanted to leave. I felt that I could continue on my own, away from the confines of the unit. But I had nowhere to go; I felt trapped. Some leave days I would go to my dad's house, other times I'd spend it with Rob. Things had improved between us and I was so glad that he seemed to be less frustrated with me. I felt that we would be okay, that I still loved him.

I watched new patients come in, which never got easier. There was one new patient that shocked me to my core. She was the thinnest person I have ever seen. She was on bed rest because she was so ill. She had to use a wheelchair to even go to the toilet. I remember looking at her and realising that she was the last category on that BMI chart. She was technically what I was aiming for. I wondered if she felt like she'd 'done it'; whether she finally felt thin. I think I knew to the answer to that, and for the first time I was glad that wasn't me. I was glad that things had changed and I was glad that I didn't get to that point. I thought about how hard it was going to be for her to even begin to recover from there. Anorexia had got her so tight in its grips, I wondered whether it would ever be possible for her to get out. I hoped so. I wished I could go and talk to her, but I didn't know what to say.

The stress of not having anywhere to live and trying to get on the council housing list was too much at times. Occasionally I cut myself or made myself sick. However, all things considered, I was doing well and trying to remain positive. I was offered a house, but it had no heating and was an absolute mess. I refused it, as I just couldn't have made that my home for recovery. I was told that my subsequent application may be refused because I had technically 'made myself homeless.' There was conflicting information, so I just had to sit and wait, which was unbearable. I wanted to leave the unit, but even if they were happy to discharge me, I wouldn't have been allowed to leave without a home to go to.

I was desperately trying to fight the boredom of hospital life, which at times is enough to drive you to the point of insanity. The better I got, the more bored I got. My brain had all this space where the anorexic thoughts had been, and I had nothing to fill it with, apart from worry. The days dragged on and on. Sometimes a day felt like a week. The same routines, the same faces, the same conversations, the same groups, the inevitable ritual of food, and always at the same times of the day. I was feeling frustrated and bored out of my mind. I wondered how I had just sat there when I was first admitted. How did I not notice this big open expanse of time that just seemed to grow and grow? I realise now that it was simply because I didn't have the brain power or functioning to notice it before, I was too engrossed in my obsession at the time; but now it was intolerable.

I had applied to study mental health nursing. Looking back, it was not the right time. But it was something I felt passionate about. I really wanted to help others. I also needed to fill that desire to 'do' and to 'achieve.' I was supposedly doing well. I'd been on the unit for some time. Lots of new patients were coming in; my original gang had slowly left. I felt that I should be better, looking to the future, trying to aim for normal things, like training in a career.

I knew I would be back out in the wild in a short time and that I should start thinking about pretending none of this had happened. I would be 'recovered' and that meant doing normal people things.

As Christmas 2007 came around, I started slipping back into thinking that I just needed to get out of the hospital and once I was out I could do it all again. I was desperately missing the comfort of anorexia. Everything felt too out of control and unorganised, unpredictable. I didn't know where I stood. I was going to go stay at my dad's over Christmas. Rob had said he wanted Christmas dinner at his parents' house. I was feeling a bit despondent about that and dreading Christmas food. While I was on leave at my dad's, I took every opportunity I could to miss a meal or a snack. When I had the house to myself I put crumbs and butter on a plate in the sink, to make it look like I had eaten. I felt that 'control' seeping back into my hands and I liked it. I felt that high and it felt good. I was 'getting one up on recovery.'

I spent the new year in Bristol with Rob and a couple of friends. Adding drugs to the mix, it was a welcome release.

When I got back to the unit, I had lost 1 kilogram, and I smiled to myself. Then I realised how much bigger I was than everyone else in the unit. I found myself sitting in morning support group listening to these tortured minds talk about how they were getting 'bigger and bigger.' I sat there thinking about how much longer I'd been there, how much more weight I'd gained. *If they were 'bigger and bigger,' what the hell was I?*

The council was dragging its feet, and it got to the point where I was seriously considering moving into a hostel, just so I could leave. I wholeheartedly believed that being in the unit with the other girls was pulling me back. I was further along in recovery and it was unbearable being surrounded by the constant reminders of anorexia day in day out.

It's hard getting used to a new body. Your clothes no longer hang off you. That was the one thing I couldn't stand. I had gotten used to my clothes fitting a certain way and measuring my 'progress' by how much looser they were. Feeling them getting tighter was almost like undoing that progress, like going backwards towards failure. Trying to convince your mind that this isn't the case is extremely difficult. Seeing as we wear clothes every day, it's a constant reminder.

Monday 21st January 2008

I look in the mirror and turn away,
How did I suddenly get this way?
It's a body I don't recognise, one I don't know,
I've lost all the work it took to show,
That inside I'm crying, shouting out,
Even though I don't know what it's all about,
So now where do I go? Which path do I take?
I should leave it behind for everyone's sake,
But sometimes deep inside, I want it back,
To gain the control that I now lack,
The control that kept me going,
That control was the only thing showing,
That I was struggling with life,
That I hurt inside,
That all these years I've been trying to hide,
By putting on a front and playing the role,
Of someone in complete control,
Why did no one notice? Why did no one see?
That I was finding it hard just to be me,
I needed something to fill that hole,
So I decided to set myself a goal,
But now that's been taken away,
I'm finding it hard every day,
To accept this new body, all the emotion,
I need to give something else the devotion,
That I gave and put in to the disorder,
But how do you start to put things in order?
That's the question I ask myself all of the time,

I just keep quietly praying that things will be fine.

At the end of January, I found out that I had a flat. A place to call my own in a good area that I knew well. It finally felt like the sun was shining down on me and I couldn't have been happier. I asked for a discharge date, which was granted. My BMI was in a place where doctors and their technical terms considered me 'healthy.' Although, of course, it was also higher than I was hoping to maintain.

I hated my body and was consumed by thoughts of getting control back, but I was just so happy to have somewhere to finally call home that for the time being those thoughts faded into insignificance. In the eyes of the unit, I was doing well. I had made great progress and my BMI was healthy. They caught me making myself sick a few times, but they didn't know that I'd actually started doing it fairly often.

I spent some time going between the hospital and my new flat. Dad helped me lay a carpet, get a washing machine, and straighten the place up. I loved those times with him; I had him to myself to talk to and just be normal. I felt like I'd not had many of these times and I really enjoyed having it be just the two of us. I found it hard when he made double-edged comments, but I brushed them off and tried to just enjoy that time.

Two days before my discharge date I found out that I had a place at university to study mental health nursing. So, I was leaving to a new home and to train in a new career.

As discharge loomed, I became more and more nervous and I realised that everything was moving at superspeed. Before I knew it, I was out. I was saying goodbye to the nurses and the patients that I'd been with day in and day out for almost five months. I was going to a new flat, on my own, and going to start at university.

My dad kept reiterating how fantastic it all was. The flat is fantastic. University is fantastic, but the pressure crushed me. Everyone kept saying it was a new year, a new start, it was all fabulous, wasn't I lucky to get the flat? It was all going to be great from here on out. Meanwhile, I wanted to scream from the top of my lungs.

Mum told me that she thought I would lose all the weight again. I disagreed. I was much better. If anything, I just wanted to lose a little bit so that I felt comfortable in my clothes; they were always a little overzealous with how much weight they wanted people to gain, weren't they? That's all it was. I was okay. I just needed to be the healthy weight that I was happy with, *not them*.

THE CLIMB BACK UP

I t was apparent that I was addicted to making myself sick. I needed the release it gave me. Rather than purging myself of food, it was as if I was trying to purge myself of bad feelings. The eating disorder unit had moved to a new building and we all had our own rooms and bathrooms. It was noted on my file that someone had to accompany me when I brushed my teeth after the final evening snack.

Around four weeks after being readmitted, I had another turn. At that point I thought I was huge and physically fine, but my body told me otherwise. All of sudden I started shaking, my ears were ringing and I was heaving uncontrollably – just like that time on my kitchen floor. The next thing I knew I had an oxygen mask on my face and a blood pressure belt attached to my arm.

My pulse had dropped and was very weak. My blood pressure had plummeted and I was lucky not to have gone into cardiac arrest. For a while my blood pressure was monitored closely. I tried to tell myself that this was a wake-up call. But the anorexia screamed in my head that they were making it into a bigger deal than it actually was, to shock me and that actually it was just a bit of a funny turn and I was perfectly fine.

This is why anorexia is deadly. It doesn't matter what happens, or what people say, that voice screams the loudest. Right up until those final fatal moments that have killed people with eating disorders, that voice will be screaming that they are fine.

I spoke to the nurse who had helped me so much before. She told me that my pulse was very low and it was a warning sign that my heart couldn't cope. She said that it was similar to angina; angina itself doesn't kill you but it's a warning that you're on the path to a heart attack. She told me that the oxygen levels in my blood were low, which is why I had felt better after the oxygen mask. She had a way of putting things that made me wonder if the voice in my head was lying to me. I suspected that I had pushed things as far as I could. Any more and I would be in real trouble.

Rob and I were just floating side by side. I didn't feel like we were really together anymore. He made excuses not to come and see me, one being that his 'coat was wet from the rain.' I felt that he didn't want to be with me and that it was all my own fault.

One day I discovered that while I was in hospital he had taken money from my account. When I questioned him about it, he told me that it was a mistake and that he had thought it was his account. I may have been blinded by the anorexia, but I was wasn't stupid. He would have had to use *my* pin number to withdraw the money. I was pleased that I had a little bit of savings, enough that I had hoped to go on holiday when, and if, this ever ended. But then I found out that the one person I trusted was stealing money from my account. What made it worse was that if he had just asked me, I would have given it to him. I didn't want yet another row, though, so I bit my tongue and brushed it under the rug.

I had to be careful on the unit who I chose to speak to. I quickly figured out which members of staff not to approach. After a pretty tough meal, I spoke to one member of staff who told me, 'try to tell yourself that you're at a healthy weight and if you lost anymore you would be underweight.' I was just over 6 stone. That really messed with my mind. I didn't know what to do with myself. Then the 'nurse of reason' arrived and once again she talked some much-needed sense in to me. She also talked about how I always want to please everyone, including the staff. She said she knew that most of the time I was just sitting there, not saying a word, even though I'm feeling something totally different. She said that it was acceptable to shout and cry and make myself known – like some of the other girls do. It really hit a nerve and brought a lump to my throat. I had an overwhelming urge to hug this woman. She always seemed to make me take a step back from myself and think.

I was getting frustrated by comments from my dad. He kept saying that I could get rid of this illness by 'being stronger.' Or that, 'if I had more things in my life, like a job, then I wouldn't have a problem.' He contradicted himself all the time, depending on whether he visited on his own or with his girlfriend. One visit, he told me that before I went into hospital, I kept putting off him visiting me, so he had known that there was something wrong. I pointed out that he had only texted me twice. He denied this with such conviction that I started to doubt myself. Had I missed phone calls and texts? These conversations left me feeling frustrated, confused and small. He seemed to believe what he was saying, and I wanted to believe him. I started to question my sanity and my mind was left in turmoil. However, deep down, I knew I was right. I have since read about the character traits of narcissism, and it very much describes his behaviour.

I knew I needed to be in hospital, but recovery was slow and the weight gain was slower than the previous admission. I was trying to find my fight and my passion for recovery. It was difficult, and I was very lonely. I didn't feel like I had any strong relationships to keep me going, to help me beat this. I knew that the fight had to come from within me; I was the only person that could do this.

My diary from this time contains another poem:

At the table

It's here with me at this table, it's watching every bite,

It's always close behind me, never out of sight,

The food in front of me smells so good,

And my body tells me that I should,

But this voice says no, tells me I'm fat,

That at this table I should not be sat,

'What the hell are you here for? What are you doing?

We should be alone together and reviewing

Your weight, your goals, where you go now

But you're sat with this food, you greedy cow

You don't need it inside you – just think where it goes!

I know you feel hungry and feel ill I suppose

But that doesn't matter! It should make you feel good!

We are heading in the direction we both know that you should!'

I try to resist and take a bite,

But it gets louder and louder, trying to kill my fight,

187

With every mouthful it just gets stronger,

Telling me I should have gone a bit longer,

Held on to the dizziness, the hunger, the pain,

Over and over it drives me insane,

With every forkful I feel guilt deep inside,

My logical side tries to override,

That noise that goes on inside my head,

From the moment I wake to when I go to bed,

The noise becomes screaming as I sit at this table,

To the point I start doubting whether I am able,

To do this, recover, to not listen and get well,

I start to believe I will be trapped in this hell,

But I do want this, it has to come from me alone,

One day I will sit at this table on my own.

During this admission my mum was having surgery on her brain tumour, which turned out to be benign, at the same hospital. I went to visit her and tried to hide the upset I felt at seeing her with her hair shaved on one side. I tried to pretend that all was normal, but obviously I was desperately worried and felt upset and guilty. It could have quite turned out to be cancerous and here I was, not eating of my own accord, *or so I told myself,* and wasting my time in hospital. I felt extremely selfish and was beating myself up tremendously. I just tried to hold on to the fact that she was okay.

The occupational therapist mentioned that I seemed to always take things on in extremes. Whether it be self-harm, food, drugs, or even over spending (at numerous points I had gotten myself into debt). She was right. I realised that these extremes came when I was feeling desperately hopeless or, actually the opposite, when I was feeling reckless. Either way, they were driven by extreme feelings. She put it down to the fact that I was trying to fill a gap. While that was partly true, it felt like there may be more to these behaviours which wasn't being explored because, after all, it was an eating disorders unit and I was too caught up in the logistics of numbers and food to put any real thought behind the moods in general.

Rob and I still had a strained relationship. I had been saving money to go on holiday with him only for him to declare that he didn't want to go. He said that our last holiday had been a disaster because of the food issue. One afternoon, out of the blue, I got a text message saying, 'Hey Sam, hope you're ok xxxxx.' Apparently, he was getting good at sending texts to the wrong person. I asked him who the hell Sam was. He told me that she was someone from the local pub, but that she was a lesbian and I didn't need to worry.

I didn't believe a word of it. He wasn't the sort of person to put kisses on the end of a text to a friend. All I got in response was, 'I didn't say I loved her, did I?!' *Well, I guess that explains everything.* I wished that if he was cheating on me he would just have the decency to finish with me. It would have been understandable, I just couldn't stand the thought of being lied to.

When I got leave, he would vanish, getting drunk and arriving back sick. I had my head in the clouds and while this made a change from the toilet, I was trying to kid myself that all was okay. I told myself that it was all my fault. I swept it all under my trusty rug and carried on planning a holiday that the dietician had already told me probably wasn't going to happen.

I carried on fighting and little by little the positive thoughts crept back in. Once again, as usual, so did the boredom and frustration. I got more leave and most of the time I didn't cope too badly, considering. I did my best and fought the thoughts as much as I could.

It was an uphill struggle and absolutely exhausting. I wondered whether it was ever going to be natural or if this is how I was going to feel forever.

Another poem from my diary at the time:

I see that girl in the mirror, looking back at me,

I see her thinking I am crazy, for believing I am free,

Yet I can see it in her eyes as I am staring,

She's trying to understand that I am not lying,

I am just trying to find my way back home to me.

***

I was struggling with my 'washing machine brain.' I was having difficulty reading and holding onto a thought for very long. It felt like the same old thoughts were just spinning in empty space.

Again, I was struggling with new patients coming in, and that I had put on about 10 kilograms in the three months I'd been in the hospital. My brain hadn't caught up with my body and all of a sudden I was back here again, without even realising that it had happened.

I carried on fighting and eating the meals. I talked to the staff more. I kept on reminding myself that this was inevitable and that I really didn't want to be doing this again.

I went against everyone's advice and went on the holiday. I had an amazing time. The sun, sea, and sand really did me the world of good. Away from the unit, I struggled with food a lot less than Rob or I thought I would. We enjoyed ourselves, for the first time in a long time.

Around six months after I was admitted for the second time, I was discharged. Once again, I was at a healthy weight and with a much healthier outlook. I remained positive and really saw a light at the end of the tunnel.

I had put university on hold, which didn't please dad much. Six months of recovery and I had managed fairly well with food. But the olanzapine medication made me insatiably hungry and I couldn't bear it, so I took myself off the medication.

I was struggling with up and down moods. I could be fine for days, like life was going great, couldn't be better, but then I'd crash. I put this down to all I'd been through and presumed it was only natural.

I started an NVQ in childcare. I thought this was a good choice, seeing as I had previously enjoyed working in nurseries. I hated being on benefits and really wanted to achieve something. This seemed like a good step. I completed the first part of the NVQ at a training centre and sought a placement to continue with the rest. However, once again, as the start date loomed so did my anxieties and that inner dialogue of perfectionism/fear of failing.

I started feeling the call to curl back up with anorexia. Those familiar feelings of guilt when I ate returned. I was determined that this wasn't going to happen again; this time it was going to be different. I couldn't do it again. Then I felt that I was pushing myself to have the 'perfect recovery' – putting pressure on myself again. I was supposed to behave like a normal human being because the scales told me I was healthy. People saw a healthy young woman who was just flailing about.

I knew that Rob and I would be over if I did this again. In the lead up to the new job, I had overwhelming anxiety. I ended up cutting, just once - I thought - just once, to rid myself of this anxiety and tension.

When I started at the nursery, I loved it with all my heart, but I felt like I stood out like a sore thumb. When I left at the end of the day, the flood gates opened on my emotions again. My moods were up, down, and all over the place. I never knew how I was going to wake up the next morning. It was very confusing. The cutting became more and more frequent, just to be able to think straight. I felt like I was walking around in a daze. I told myself that I would be fine. That this was better than going back to anorexia and that it would pass.

I was in a job, behaving like a normal human. I thought that I just had to carry on ... and then maybe the way I was portraying myself would become my reality.

BLACK AND BETRAYAL

The shadows were hunting me. I was trying to dodge them at every turn; trying to tell myself that I was normal, everything was fine. This was just normal life and how things were. Everyone had a chaotic brain, right? I no longer had anorexia as an excuse for dodging life, so I tried to throw myself into what I thought was recovery.

Things hadn't been great between Rob and I since the holiday. We'd had such a lovely time, but 10 minutes after we got back, he was on his phone again. I felt so gutted. I felt like we were growing apart. I was upset and confused; I had really believed that being free from anorexia would change things and get us back to where we once were, but that didn't seem to be the case.

One day, he came to the flat and announced that he had something to tell me. He told me that there was a girl at work that had taken a liking to him and that she had tried to blackmail him. He told me that she had seen him at the pub and told him he had to text her or she was going to go to the police and tell them he had tried to rape her. It turned out that it was the day we came back from holiday and that was why he was on his phone so soon. His dad wanted to meet him to warn him that the police were coming, they had been waiting for us to get back. I had been totally oblivious and couldn't believe my ears. I also couldn't get my head around why this would be a problem. Surely, he should have just told her to go ahead because nothing had happened? But he spun me a line and I believed it. It didn't occur to me for one second that there was anything in the claim. I was mad at this girl ... after everything I'd been through, how dare she get a silly crush and try to ruin our lives. I didn't have any reason to question this man who I loved and had spent six years of my life with.

I tried to push it under the ever-protruding rug. I felt like I was drowning. I started to feel like I couldn't breathe under the black smog that was filling my lungs. I clung to my job, even though I was finding it more and more difficult to drag myself out of bed in the morning. I scraped a smile across my face trying not to show what was happening. *I was slipping.*

One day a co-worker approached me and asked if I was okay. I tried to make out that I was fine, but it was obvious that I wasn't. I felt like I was walking through treacle. Every step was heavy and every smile physically hurt. By the time I got home each night, I was exhausted from the pretence. I would cry with frustration and inevitably end up cutting. I was walking around in a daze, just pretending to live. The days passed in a blur of false pretence.

One day, I was called into the office at work with the other trainees. We were told that two of us had to be let go. My heart sank. This job was all that was holding me together. This was what showed I had normal life. Without it I'd have nothing. I'd have failed all over again.

They told us that we would be re-interviewed, and the manager would make her decision. In the lead up to the interview, my overly anxious mind went in to overdrive. The usual self-doubt took over my mind.

As it turned out, the interview went well. I was told how good I was at my job and I was one of the three staff that stayed. I was so relieved that I didn't need to feel like a failure, but I still could not lift myself out of the black. It was there, whichever way I turned, and I felt like it was never going to go away - no matter what I did or however how much I tried.

Monday 31st August 2009

I seriously don't know what's the matter with me, there's not even a reason for me to feel like this, I'm just so... I don't even know! All I know is that one minute I'm okay. In fact, at times, everything is great! For a few days it's like life couldn't be better and then – bang - I feel awful again. It hits me and I worry about everything, I wonder why anyone bothers with me and I cut myself to pieces to try and stop the buzzing in my head I never know when it's going to hit.

I am so tired and so drained of being like this. Is my brain wired wrong or something? Is it me?

I don't want to go to work tomorrow, which is stupid because I love it but I'm putting on a show of being fine and I barely have the energy to do it anymore. My nerves are hanging by a thread just trying to carry on like everything is normal, the life I am portraying is fake.

I don't even know how to explain what I'm feeling apart from that I feel like I have so much to say but really there's nothing there? I know that doesn't make sense, but that's the only way I can explain it.

Sometimes I have to stop myself from just cutting and cutting and cutting until... I don't know. I don't want to die but I don't want to live either; this isn't living anyway.

Those feelings built up more and more. I was either feeling great or suicidal. There was no in-between. My brain was moving quickly but my body waded through treacle. The frustration caused by this was out of this world. I spent so much time at home trying to resist the urge to smash the whole place up.

Monday 7th September 2009

I'm so anxious all the time, to the point that I don't know what to do with myself. I don't even know how I'm keeping it together at work. People have started to notice, I keep thinking about taking a load of tablets. I can't live with this amount of noise in my brain.

I feel like nothing is heading anywhere, it's all so slow and nothing means anything, even though logically I know that this is nonsense. Most of what I think I know is nonsense but most of the time it all moves around my head so fast I don't have time to grasp how I'm feeling. Every tiny little thing is making me jump out of my skin at the moment. Every little noise seems amplified somehow. I just don't know what's going on.

Rob also had a meeting with his solicitor and barrister and I've been worried all day. I asked him what they said and all I got in response was, 'it isn't bad, but I don't want to talk about it.' Well maybe I would - maybe I would like to know what the hell is going on!

He stormed out and I got a text saying, 'thanks, all I wanted was a hug and to chill a bit.' Now he's ignoring my texts and my calls. Can't he see that I'm scared and I just want to know what's going on?

It didn't occur to me to doubt the story he'd told me. I didn't have the brain space to question it. The case was to heard at the crown court. I tried to pretend that it wasn't happening and to tell myself that this was just a silly little girl with a crush. Rob wasn't like my dad. This was the man I'd spent six years of my life with. He wasn't that sort of person. This would all just go away on its own.

He later changed his plea to guilty. He told me that he did it for leniency, but that meant that he would have to sign the sex offenders register. I couldn't believe what was happening. I couldn't cope with the idea that all the men in my life were involved in this sort of stuff. I tried desperately to block it out. I managed fairly successfully to not think about it, but only on a surface.

At the beginning of July 2009, my mind skewed. It started with me feeling suicidal. I was crying all the time and nothing could lift me. One night I went to bed and woke up full of adrenaline. It was like someone had flicked the 'on' switch and there was electricity in my veins. It was an anxiety fuelled energy that I didn't know what to do with. Everywhere I turned, there was so much that needed to be done, but if I tried to think of what these things were there was actually nothing. It was almost like a physical 'sparking' of two wires in my brain.

I wasn't sleeping well; I kept waking in the night feeling as though I had been asleep for hours. I often got up between 2.00am–4.00am. Everything had to be *now*. Even that was too slow. Everyone around me was slow, I felt like I needed to wind them all up. My brain was moving too fast and I was finding it difficult to hold onto one thought. I felt like I needed to keep talking because everything was spinning around so quickly in my head. I didn't want to go to bed, I felt like I might miss something important.

One night, I got into bed but couldn't keep still. It was like jumping jacks had taken over my body and I couldn't stop fidgeting. Rob looked at me curiously as I laughed uncontrollably over some little thing. Then I felt an incredible energy. It felt like I was on drugs. It felt amazing, like nothing could stop me. I was invincible; I was running from room to room, smiling, singing, cleaning and talking to myself in the mirror. I didn't want the feeling to end. It was complete euphoria. It was non-drug induced and I told myself how well I was, how far I'd come from those depressive feelings.

I was doing everything at super speed, but it felt slow. I remember sitting with my laptop and feeling like I was in a warped time zone. Everything seemed surreal. I started typing. I remember watching my fingers move quickly but it was like it was being played in a strange slow motion. I watched random videos on YouTube and found myself wondering what the people's names were or what they did for living. One woman in particular caught my attention. I decided that her name began with 'J' and I went through every possible name. I pondered all the things

I could do. I considered going for a run. My brain was spinning so fast that it felt like my head may very well just fly off my shoulders.

Inevitably this didn't last. Things started to slow down, and I was left feeling frustrated.

Every little thing was making me jump. I started to think that evil was in me. I decided the way to beat this evil was to sleep in the living room with the lights on. That way it wouldn't be able to get me, I thought. Not that I was really sleeping anyway. I started pacing a lot. I didn't know what to do with myself. It went on this way for two weeks, and by the end I couldn't even have the TV on because it just sounded so loud, like it was piercing my brain. So much as a flickering street lamp would set me off feeling agitated. If Rob tried to calm me down, I would physically push him and tell him to fuck off. I shouted at shop staff for no apparent reason. I was out of control. It felt like I was crawling in my own skin and I wanted to tear it off piece by piece.

Over the next few weeks my moods deteriorated and there was no way to pull myself back. I had gone to a place of no return. All I wanted to do was end my life. I no longer wanted to be a member of this cruel world that had nothing to offer but pain and fighting for a freedom that I was never going to experience. It was too much. Way too much.

One Monday, I had an appointment at the eating disorder unit. My usual doctor was out sick, so I had to see another doctor. He asked me questions and I answered minimally. I couldn't focus and all I could think about was that I wanted to kill myself. The questions were pointless and so was answering them.

After the I appointment I went back to my nan's house. On the bus ride home she was talking to me, but I had no idea what she was saying. I just nodded where I thought it was appropriate. I was thinking about going home and cutting myself, smashing my flat to smithereens and taking an overdose. It was starting to feel inevitable. Like I was just waiting for the right time and I would be free. Walking home from my nan's, I felt like I wasn't even there. I felt I might almost disappear in to thin air. 'Poof' and I'd be gone. It was very surreal. I walked along looking at my feet, counting the steps, telling myself that if I could logically count my steps in sequence it would all be okay. I knew something was wrong in my head, so I did something I'd never usually do: I rang the doctor for an emergency appointment. I decided to ask for help.

I walked into the appointment and it all exploded from my mouth: I didn't care if I died; I wanted to die; all the crazy stuff I had been thinking; Rob and his case, why I couldn't bear it because of things my dad had done; that I was feeling out of control. He looked at me and asked how I felt about sex. I told him that I had always had issues with it. I didn't enjoy it like other people. It made me feel uncomfortable and I had always just gone through the motions because I thought that's what I should do. He then proceeded to spend the whole appointment telling me that I was very attractive, I had a pretty face, nice hair, nice smile, lovely eyes. He started asking more questions about my sex life and said that maybe it wasn't me the problem lay with. It went on and on. I was left feeling distraught and uncomfortable. I thought at the time that maybe he was trying to make me feel better, make me realise that I was okay. Looking back, I realise that this wasn't the case.

I had taken a lot of time off work. I couldn't face people, the job, or even getting myself there. I couldn't concentrate, and I would have been no use. People were already looking at me oddly and asking me what was wrong.

I went in one day feeling like maybe I could get through it, only to be told that they weren't happy with me because I wasn't following the correct procedure for time off. They said I was brilliant at my job but that I 'obviously had a chip on my shoulder,' that I was always looking for something to criticise and was very negative. I broke down and explained how I'd been feeling. I said that I was stressed and told them about Rob's impending trial.

My doctor had called my workplace and expressed his concerns about my welfare. He also raised concerns with my local team, as I was suicidal. In my mind, suicide was inevitable. There was no way that it wasn't going to happen. I day-dreamed about pills. I stashed them away for when the day came.

Every morning, I woke up asking myself 'what do I have to wake up for?' I remember lying there for 40-minutes one morning, not moving a muscle as I listened to the ticking of the clock wondering if I would disappear if I lay there and listened to it long enough.

I hung on, as I was due a visit from the local mental-health team. I reasoned that I would see if they could help me, and if not, I would start planning how I w end it.

I have various scraps of paper with the scribblings of a very chaotic mind from this time. They are nothing like my previous diary entries; they aren't even in order. They're just random notes from random times. I was trying to make sense of what was going on around me. There are lists of who I needed to write goodbye notes to. I wanted to be ready for when I finally took my own life. This period is a bit of a blur, like my mind had melted. It had taken too much pressure and started to disintegrate.

I went through another period of 'sparking' in my mind. I'm not religious, but I got it into my head that God was watching over me. I felt full of electricity, but this was different, it was scary electricity. I didn't know what to do with myself. I couldn't sit down; I couldn't sit still; I couldn't think. My thoughts were like lots of singular words joined in random sentences that didn't make sense.

I thought my flat was full of evil. The evil was in droplets that touched all the surfaces and they were trying to infect me. I thought the only way to stop this from happening was to put crosses with masking tape all over my walls; then I would be safe. I bleached all the surfaces to get rid of the droplets and taped crosses all over my living room wall, but it wasn't enough. It was spreading. I couldn't control it and I had no idea what to do.

In a blind panic I phoned the eating disorder unit and asked to speak to my doctor. I blurted out something that I'm sure didn't make much sense. I can't remember exactly what I said, apart from that I couldn't get out of the flat because of the evil droplets and that I was trapped. I remember his voice telling me that I was okay and that it would be okay; I should just stay there and not go out, he would send someone to me.

I remember having a meeting in the hospital after I had almost taken an overdose. I can't remember exactly how it happened, but one minute I was having a meeting and the next minute I was inpatient again. This wasn't the eating disorder unit with the friendly faces that I'd become accustomed to, this was a general adult psychiatric unit - *and it terrified me to my bones.*

Monday 5th October 2009

I can't believe that I'm writing this, but I'm inpatient again. Not in the eating disorder unit, but on a general psychiatric ward. I'm so fucking scared! I'm too scared to get a drink, too scared to eat, too scared to go in the day room. I rang my mum, who rang the unit, probably because she worried about me not eating. The nurse bought the phone in to me and snapped, 'why have you not eaten?' Before I could say that the doctor was talking to me, she said, 'we offered you a sandwich, why did you say no?' I told her that I had felt flustered and like I was being a pain. She rolled her eyes and snapped, 'you need to tell the truth, we are having problems with your mum.' I was then in the middle of explaining to my mum on the phone, trying not to cry, and she held out her hand and said, 'thank you, this is the office phone.'

I feel so alone and scared. I've literally just been sitting here shaking. I rang Rob and he told me to just ignore her, that not everyone will be nice. Does he not understand how terrifying this is? That the very first person to come in to my room made me feel like even more of an inconvenience? I wish the ground would swallow me up right now. I need some support. I need some help. I feel like I've been tossed somewhere just so I don't kill myself. I'm in limbo, complete f*cking limbo. I understand the meaning of that word all too well now.

I've just been told that supper is ready but I'm too scared to even go in. How pathetic am I? I wish I could shrivel up and never have existed. That way I would have never lived, never kept myself alive for other people, never loved someone with the whole of my heart and therefore never hurt, and me dying wouldn't hurt anyone... that sounds perfect.

I was determined to leave the following day. I summoned the courage to go to breakfast and found one of the girls from the eating disorder unit sitting at the table. I was so relieved to see a familiar face that it settled some of the nerves. This was a new territory for me. It was the sort of place that people go in films. It was nothing like the eating disorder unit, there were no groups or anything like that. I remember looking around thinking that it seemed like a place just to preserve life. People were there because they were thought to be a danger to themselves or other people.

My mum spoke to my doctor at the eating disorder unit. He told her that I was welcome to go see him, but that I was now under the care of the doctor in the psychiatric ward. I should wait to see her, and she would prescribe me medication. I was crushed; I had trusted that man with my life, and I didn't trust people very often.

I saw an American doctor who just sat and looked at me like I was a fraud, like he wondered what I was even doing there. He said, 'well I don't think you're mentally ill, so you can leave if you want.' He told me that self-harm was child's play and that I had never done any serious harm to myself, right? Why hadn't I? I told him that I did it to release my frustration and emotions, that I would hate to have to go to a hospital. He looked at me and asked, 'so you don't like that sort of attention?' He told me that when I say I feel like killing myself everyone panics and says that I must stay in hospital, but I'd never actually done anything, had I?

I could feel myself sinking, I felt like a worthless insect on the bottom of his shoe.

He went on to talk about Rob's upcoming court case. He said, 'anybody would be devastated, but you look like you don't care. Doesn't it piss you off that he was texting a 15-year-old girl? If I did that, my girlfriend would turn on her heels.' He pushed it further, telling me that it couldn't be just texting, things like that don't go to court.' I told him that he wouldn't lie to me and he simply looked at me and said, 'men do lie to their partners.' I lost it. I fled the room, punched my wardrobe repeatedly, and was in hysterics. I phoned my mum, who called the ward and went ballistic.

The way he had been going on was just like what my dad did. Wearing me down, confusing my struggling brain. He confirmed all the horrible things I already felt about myself. The things that other people were telling me to fight against. Who was I supposed to believe? I was getting conflicting messages and feelings from every angle. I had no one to trust. No one to give me a solid piece of advice. I couldn't even trust myself. I had nowhere to turn and I wanted to die. At that point, that was all I wanted. I wanted to cease to exist.

People like him should not be allowed to be a doctor, let alone go near someone with a mental illness. In spite of him, I decided to do the sensible thing and stay. I would wait to see the actual doctor when she returned. Maybe she could give me some answers, at least some medication to sort out my hectic brain.

My mum rang work to say that I wouldn't be in. My manager called asking what was wrong. I told her that I had had a difficult weekend and was waiting for a phone call for an appointment. In my mind, there was no way I could be honest about the state I was in. I was hoping it would be a quick fix and that I'd be back at work before they suspected that anything was seriously wrong. All she kept asking was whether there was any way I could come in. I said I couldn't, and she asked why I couldn't just go to work and to tell them to call the work phone. My exhausted brain hadn't thought this through properly. She kept asking me what exactly was going on, that she needed to know, that she needed me at work. I made my excuses because there was no way I could say to her, 'actually

I'm in a psychiatric hospital so I can't make it today … sorry about that.'

In the back of my mind, I knew I was going to lose this job. My attempt at 'normal' was, once again, a total failure. My manager was off until Monday, so I knew I had until then to work out some kind of plan.

Thursday 8th October 2009

I had ward rounds today and Jesus Christ! It's nothing like the eating disorder unit ward round. There were so many people in there; I didn't know what to do with myself! I felt like an absolute idiot and I'm pretty sure they thought the same. They asked how things were and so I told the truth. I also told them about the self-harming. They told me to go to them if I feel like doing it, but that they will leave it as my responsibility, which is perfectly fine by me.

I was asked afterwards by the nurse who admitted me how I feel about being here because she thinks they want me to stay another week.

It seems that they concluded in ward round that my problems are Rob, Dad, and work, and that without these I would be okay, but I wouldn't. These things have not helped, but they aren't the make or break of my whole life.

My manager is back at work on Monday too, so somehow I'm going to have to explain all of this. I don't even know if I'm going to be able to go back to work. Why do I keep messing up?

I agreed to stay a little longer. I figured that as much as I wanted to die, this was my last chance, so I may as well see if they could help me. Maybe they would be able to give me some answers, or something that could help. I decided to cling to that little ray of hope.

MISPLACED DEVOTION

One week in hospital turned into nearly three months.

I battled with my sanity and with the people around me. My dad continued to be an issue and even the ward began to notice. My lovely, caring nurse wanted to refuse him entry because every time he visited I was left a mess. His words twisted my head inside out. He was constantly going on about Rob and what he'd done; my mind was screaming about how hypocritical he was.

I told him that they were allocating me a psychologist and he texted me: 'I think they will just try and get you to make yourself better. It's all in your head. You can make a start as soon as you want, you know, by deciding to make a change and stop wasting your life in hospital by enjoying your life and your flat and your job instead? You have the choice you know, surely you don't need a psychologist to tell you that lol, you are a smart girl? You're just making stupid decisions lately but hey, we can all do that lol.'

I texted him backing saying that if he felt like that then fine. I hadn't chosen to be in hospital for a bloody holiday. His reply was, 'obviously we see it differently then don't we? But then that's probably the reason you're in there.' I told him that if that's how he felt then I don't know why he bothers to come and see me. In response, I simply got: 'I'm sorry you feel like that.'

I tried to play him at his own game and text back that I was sorry that he felt the way he did too. I thought that was it, because I didn't hear back for a while. Later, I received this: 'I've rechecked the texts we have sent each other today and I can see no reason why you would speak to me like that. All through this illness, and the last couple of years in fact, the only people to have really stood by you is me and your nan. Everyone else has come and gone, lasted a few visits, haven't visited you much, not even bothered to help you in your flat. Has anyone else painted or laid carpets or done anything for you? And you think it's ok to talk to me like that when I've done nothing but love and support you? Good grief Katie, I know you are ill but do I really deserve that?'

When I got that text I felt as if my stomach had been ripped out. Was he right? Was I a terrible daughter? On the one hand, he's saying that it's all in my head, but with the next breath he's saying that I'm ill. I didn't know what to believe. I wanted to love him. I wanted a dad. I felt as though that he was trying to confuse me on purpose, but then I felt guilty and wondered if he believed what he was saying and really believed that was being a bitch. *Maybe I was?*

The crux of the matter is that he emotionally manipulated me. He did it very well. He always came out on top, leaving everyone else to question themselves. He did it to my mum too, he sold my nan's husband a car that wasn't his to sell, all the police trouble and accusations. Yet he would never admit it. To this day, I doubt he'd admit it. He'd deny it and maybe even believe what he was saying. It would be everyone else's fault. I was ill and didn't know what I was saying, and mum was manipulative and crazy. I don't know how he would account for all the other stories that I've heard from people. No doubt he would find a way, and it would be convincing. Charming, almost. It messed with my head, but it also broke my heart. I wanted to love him, and I wanted him to love me. I desperately wanted to be a good daughter.

I had taken a pin from the corkboard in the unit and squirreled it away in my pocket. It was all I had, but it was something. When things got to be too much, I would scratch at my skin over and over and over. It was noticed; I was put on higher observation, and eventually, it was taken from me.

I made a couple of friends, but mostly I kept to myself. Patients were pretty much left to their own devices. There were no structured groups or activities, and time passed like Groundhog Day, waiting for ward rounds and one to ones with nurses. My nurse was a superstar; he was lovely and kind and I was thankful that I had him.

On the unit, it was easy to go unnoticed. Attention was directed to those kicking off or trying to escape. People were regularly wrestled to the floor by staff, or worse still, if someone was really kicking off, an alarm would ring and people ran in from all sides, using force to get people to the floor. For someone like me, who just wanted to be left alone, it was easy to fade into the background.

I hadn't told anyone about my 'buzzing' experiences. I only mentioned that my brain felt like it was on a spin cycle. I was too embarrassed to try to explain it properly, and I was scared of what they would think. It was easier to speak about the depression; I was put on fluoxetine, an antidepressant.

Shortly after, the 'buzzing' brain came back. My mind sped up. One evening, I sat looking at my multicoloured jelly bean diary cover and became lost in it. I couldn't believe that I hadn't noticed how beautiful it was before. It was like magic, utter magic. I imagined myself jumping into it. Jumping into those colours and being totally immersed in a rainbow of jelly beans. I thought about how it held the answers to everything. If I could get inside this cover, inside the rainbow, I'd know life's answers.

I went outside for a cigarette and looked at the sky. It was beautiful. The stars were beautiful. You could see them all, and that was almost definitely a sign, because it's rare to see the stars these days, I thought. It's always cloudy, always foggy, there's always fog clouding all the answers. But not tonight, they are all there for the taking. My mind was flying. I couldn't catch a thought; they were flitting from topic to topic. My brain tried to attach a rhyme to everything I looked at: the grass, the wall, the lights. The rhymes span in my mind and I tried to keep up. I got frustrated when I looked at an ambulance and couldn't for the life of me think of anything to rhyme with it. That ruined the whole flow.

I savoured these moments and hoped they would last. Inevitably, they always ended in agitation and frustration a few days later. This was followed by depression and the sinking black hole that swallowed me up once again.

I never told anyone about these times. I may have skimmed the surface, but I never fully explained them. I thought people would think I was making it up or that I was indeed bat-shit crazy.

I became tired, tired of the fight, tired of pretending, tired of being me. I started telling my mum and Rob that I was fine because I was sick of talking. It felt pointless. I was tired of speaking words, empty, meaningless words that amounted to nothing. I had lost my fight. I'd clung onto that tiny ray of hope that there must me something or someone, somewhere that could help me. I was concluding that this wasn't the case. There was nothing and there was no one. I was in this alone and I didn't have the fight left in me.

Suicide seemed like a full-fledged option. It made sense. The only thing that stopped me was hurting Rob, Mum, and Nan. I wished that I had no family, no one to hurt, so that I could slip off and put myself out of my misery. The guilt of hurting people more than I already had kept me floating from one empty day to the next.

One day, I spent five hours curled up on my hospital bed thinking about ways to kill myself. I didn't even notice it had been that long until I realised that it was dark outside. No one noticed. No one asked if I was okay. It was fine by me. I couldn't bear conversation anyway.

I was, however, genuinely touched when a mutual friend of mine and Rob's, who I didn't see all that often, told me that he wasn't happy with the help I was getting at the unit. He emailed a private clinic to enquire about NHS funding. It never went anywhere, but the fact that he had thought to do that deeply touched me.

I was put on lorazepam – a benzodiazepine that is prescribed for many reasons, but predominantly anxiety. I immediately loved it. At first, it made me sleep, which was all I wanted. Then, once I got used it, it chilled me out. It either calmed my whizzing brain or made me feel tranquil, which wasn't something I was used to feeling. Whenever I started to feel myself getting wound up, I asked for one. Everything slowed down. I felt calmer and my heart felt like it was beating at a normal rhythm.

I was told in the ward-round that my medication was being changed to mood stabilisers because antidepressants weren't working. I didn't really understand the change or how mood stabilisers were different, but at this point I didn't really care. I was told that I would see the inpatient psychologist and that they wanted me to stay until Rob's court case was over. They wanted to see whether anything changed once that had been dealt with. I told her that I felt like I was a pain being there – that I was just a nuisance. She replied that it wasn't the ideal place for me, but that the ideal place for me didn't exist... translate that as you will!

I was dreading telling my dad that I was going to be staying longer. I didn't want to disappoint him, and

I couldn't bear any more confusion. I knew that as soon as I told him he would be on his way.

Thursday 15th October 2009

Well dad's been and gone and I feel like shit. I've cried a lot, but I haven't got the right to cry because he loves me and wants what's best for me, I can see it in his eyes. I get confused by things that he says, like I asked him If I had let him down and he just said, 'you've let yourself down; that's more important.' He looked so sad; I love him so much. I don't want to upset him.

He was going on about Rob again and that his family were white trailer trash, that I was gullible and I would never be happy with him. He told me that my step-mum had texted him saying sorry that I was ill again and that she found out because Rob's dad was talking to someone where she was.

He looked at me and said, 'they are all laughing and gossiping behind my princess' back.'

I feel so guilty. He told me that he'd broken his finger, how could I not have known that??

Before he left I told him that I was sorry. I didn't tell him straight away that I would be staying there for a while. I didn't want to upset him, and he just said, 'well that upsets me.' I texted him later and said that I was sorry and I loved him and all I got back was, 'so am I.' So I texted back and said that he had nothing to be sorry for and he said, 'well I'm not too sure about that but let's just concentrate on getting you better.'

My head was fucked-up. I found my razor stash and cut, it made me feel a little better. Well, made me feel less like smashing my head against the wall.

This diary entry still upsets me. I read it with a desperate need to tell my former self to wake up and smell the roses. This wasn't my fault. I wasn't a bad person. And it wasn't acceptable for this man, who I loved dearly, to be treating me this way.

These conversations were an emotional torture. I didn't know what to think or what to believe. Did he love me? Did he hate me? Was he concerned about me? Was he ashamed of me? I would think one thing, then in the next breath he took it away and replaced it with the opposite feeling. He would say that it was in my head and that I was choosing to have a holiday in the unit (believe you me, if it was a holiday destination, there'd be a lot of people wanting refunds) Then, with the next breath, he would tell me that we needed to concentrate on getting me better. Then telling me that people were laughing at me and gossiping behind my back. He was so good at these subtle mind games. I became convinced that it was my fault.

Regardless, I was devastated that I hadn't noticed that he had broken his finger. I felt like the worst person in the world. He was like my anorexia: I tried desperately to please him, for him to be happy with me, but it was never enough. I was trapped in the false belief that he wanted the best for me. I'm sure in his own way he probably did – unlike the anorexia – but the relationship itself was just as toxic to me.

I texted my step-mum to ask her about the conversation she had with Rob's dad. She told me he had been genuinely concerned for me and that in nobody was gossiping or laughing at me.

She went on to say that she couldn't believe what was happening with Rob. I asked her what she had been told (I hadn't said anything). She told me that dad had told her he'd been charged with incitement of a minor between the ages of 13-15 and that he had tried to force a 13-year-old to have anal sex with him. That wasn't true. He had been charged with incitement of a minor and there was an impending court case, but the rest of it wasn't true. Once again, I was left wondering why dad always felt the need to twist things. I also wondered why I always felt so awful when I was with him. Why did my stomach twist itself into knots? Why did I never feel good enough? Why did I get so unbearably upset if I thought I had upset him? I worried about upsetting other people too, but with him it was a whole different ball game.

My self-harming continued. The unit wasn't on top of what was going on inside its walls – especially with the quieter patients. It got bad and the cuts covered the tops of my thighs. The sting would keep me going, until it faded; then I'd do it again. It was like

I needed a constant reminder that I was, in fact, alive. If I had a particularly bad day, I'd cut on top of the cuts that hadn't even begun to heal.

One day, my dad came to see me with his partner. She looked like a rabbit caught in the headlights. Up against a wall, with tears in her eyes, she looked around and told me that I didn't need to be in a place like this. She was quite well to do, a head teacher, and most probably had never encountered this kind of environment before. If you looked through to the lounge area, there was a lady sat with a tea towel on her head. A woman poked their head around the door, looked at me, and shouted at me to 'go back to my own country.' I have always had tanned skin and when I go on holiday there's always a point where some local speaks to me a language I don't understand, mistaking me for Spanish or Greek. My mum is the same, so when she visited me and we were together, the woman would linger in the doorway. I was used to her, but I guess if you've never been exposed to these situations it's a bit of a culture shock!

Dad's girlfriend looked at me and asked, 'so, what are they doing in here, apart from sedating you?' Dad stood there, looking like a totally broken man. I felt the usual guilt wash over me, although I wondered how much of it was for her benefit.

Broken or not, he still managed to come out with some fantastic lines. They were a little more dumbed down when he was with her, but they were still like some kind of brain teaser: 'we don't have to be someone if we don't like that person, we can choose a role model.'

Was this some kind of theory that he had decided to live by? It was bizarre, even by my standards. I wondered what went on in his head. As for a role model, who on earth would I choose? Him? I was surrounded by anything but role models. Even if I decided I wanted one, I wouldn't have known where to start.

He told me how well I was doing before this hospital admission and I realised how little he knew me. I had been anything but good. I was living a lie. It portrayed nothing of how I felt most of the time.

Dad's girlfriend piped up again to share another pearl of misplaced wisdom: she told me about how one of her teaching assistants also had 'problems', but that she hadn't ended up in the hospital. Rage was bubbling inside me. This woman knew nothing about me whatsoever, she knew nothing about my life. I had woken up that morning angry, looking for a fight, and it took all of my energy not to swing at her. It was probably a good thing that I had started my new medication, because it made me feel tired and my brain felt like it resembled cotton wool. Thank God, the conversation shifted.

Unfortunately, it shifted to recent goings on in the news. There was a story about a nursery nurse who had been convicted for child pornography. I looked at dad and he said that it was 'awful and disgusting.' I looked back at his partner, who was agreeing vehemently. I almost felt sorry for her. This woman was a headteacher, she was well educated, yet she was completely taken in by him. She had no clue, yet she stood there judging me for my issues and for being in the hospital. While I felt sorry for her, I was also secretly glad that she was here, in the hospital, and clearly feeling uncomfortable.

Guilt was still the overbearing feeling I had towards my dad. He looked so sad. But there was also something slightly different in his eyes. I wondered if it was because I was starting to look at him differently, starting to realise what he was all about, *and he knew it.*

After they left, his girlfriend sent me a text message, telling me what all this was doing to my dad. *What it was doing to Dad?* Once again, I ended up in tears and the same familiar knot residing in my stomach.

I was thinking more and more about suicide. I had nothing left to keep me going. I believed that I had lost my fight. I was due to leave the hospital in one week, and I felt awful. Nothing was going to help me.

In the ward round, I was given a review sheet stating that I was feeling better, that I have less suicidal thoughts and I didn't want to go home until after Rob's court case. I wasn't sure whether this was what they believed, or what I had portrayed (I was very good at feeling one thing and then opening my mouth, only to give the opposite impression).

I'd had to tell my NVQ assessor to put my course on hold. I was literally weeks away from finishing it, but there was nothing I could do about it at that point. Of course, now I felt like I had failed that too. My job was still on hold, but I knew it was coming very close to the day where that wasn't going to be the case.

Sunday 25th October 2009

I haven't been eating very much. What's the point? I'm sick of being told that I'm a 'pretty girl', a 'clever girl', that people look at me and assume from the outside that I'm okay, that my life is rosy (or that it should be). It's not and it never has been. I'm just too good at my front, at my face, at giving others help and advice while pretending that I'm fine. I have decent clothes, my hair is done most of the time, and I wear makeup most of the time, even if inside I want to die. So, people assume that I'm okay, while inside I feel black and knotted. It's all tucked nicely away in my head to the point where it's starting to explode. I want to cut myself until the blood pours out, but I don't; I want to scream and smash things, but I don't; instead I lock myself away and don't say a word. I cut myself, just enough to hurt but never enough to cause damage to the extent that it will need the involvement of other people. I make sure I'm alone when I cry, I smile, I'm polite. Anything as to not cause attention, because I'd be embarrassed, because I feel like an attention seeker. I think that's what people think, so I try not to draw attention to it. I don't want people to see me at my worst, so I do my best to contain it. Who the hell would I want to create more reasons to feel embarrassed and hate myself even more than I already do?

I think this is how a lot of people within the system are missed. Too many people vanish and end their lives. I was told more than a few times by various medical professionals over the years that I, 'looked nice and was obviously taking care of myself.' There is no 'obviously' about it. It should not be assumed that because someone is presenting a certain way, that is how they are: that if someone is wearing nice clothes, they have makeup on and their hair is done, that they are somehow no longer a risk because they can function enough to go through these routines.

Don't get me wrong, for the most part I didn't wear makeup in my darkest times, but other times I did. They call makeup war paint for a reason! In my case, even if I am very depressed, I will continue to attempt to make myself look presentable. I think that if I can just carry on putting my face on, quite literally, and if I manage to make myself *look* like a functioning human being, then maybe I will somehow become one. Too often – and this is not just from my own experience – this is taken to be an indication that someone is okay. I, and other people I know, have purposely gone to certain appointments without makeup or tidy hair because we know that we will get taken more seriously. That's messed up. That shouldn't be the case. A bit of makeup and a hairstyle shouldn't be a factor.

When I was under 6 stone and in the hospital for anorexia I still did my hair and makeup, and I was still putting on fake tan! Did this mean that I wasn't really under 6 stone? That I wasn't ill and slowly killing myself? No. It meant that I was attempting to be me, to cling on to some normality, to keep up a front, to show the world, and myself, that I was okay.

I took razors into the unit and boxes of tablets that I stashed in my clothes in the wardrobe. They never did bag checks after leave like they were supposed to. I once disappeared into town without their permission and went back to my flat for a couple of hours. No one ever rang me or said anything when I got back. I assume that they hadn't even noticed.

The only real ray of light in that hospital was my assigned nurse, who was genuinely lovely and he talked to me when I needed him to.

My course was on hold, but I felt the pressure of the job looming over me, and, of course, Rob's court date. My mum had told me that putting my course on hold was the best thing to do while I sort myself out. Then she spoke to one of her friends, who told her that I needed a focus, so all of a sudden she was telling me that she thought I should go back to work the following week when I left the hospital. I felt so confused and I was sick of conflicting messages. I felt that no one had a clue what to do with me, that I was just a lost cause. I felt that the only person who understood me was Rob; I was praying that he wouldn't be taken away from me.

My mood continued to peak and trough. Sometimes I would feel better - almost excited - other times I would feel a suicidal depression. I managed to keep both contained, without any one really being any the wiser.

One night, after a few days of feeling 'better,' which I assumed was the medication working, I remember watching the TV and starting to feel a little jittery. I began to realise how amazing the TV was. The detail. I can remember it quite clearly. The colours, the patterns, it was incredible and I sat watching it in absolute awe. I turned to one of my inpatient friends and asked if she'd turned up the TV, to which she gave me a quizzical look. It was like HD x 100. I nattered on telling the person next to me that I could get up and go to work with no problem and that I was going to be absolutely fine. It was like being on cocaine. It felt amazing.

Once again, it didn't last. I was thrown back into the depths of darkness. At the same time, I found out that Rob's court case had been postponed three weeks. My mum told me that if I was going to carry on having Rob and my dad in my life, I would have to put up with everything that came with it. I was devastated that she was being like that. I desperately wanted some support. To me, this was the man I'd been with nearly six years and my *dad*; I didn't feel like I could just disown them. I could tell that she was frustrated by the situation, and that there was nothing anyone could say to make it better. I felt like I was a complete burden and a drain on everybody's soul.

I decided to try and explain to dad how his comments were upsetting me. When he next texted me about visiting, I told him that I was finding his visits hard because I constantly thought that I was letting him down or that he thought I was just doing it for attention. He replied saying that he never implied that and never even thought it, until now, but just because I had said it. He aid that I just didn't listen or believe what he says, so he would keep his mouth shut from here on out. He said he would tell me that he loved me and leave it at that. I left terribly upset and confused.

I was told that my mood stabilisers were to be increased. It was a different doctor; I felt at ease with her. I confided in her about the 'strange' periods I'd been experiencing. I asked her if she knew what they might be about? She totally avoided my question and I was left feeling like an idiot for finally opening up about it. I felt that she thought I was attention seeking, and that was also what I had become to believe that everyone thought of me

I carried on, going back to my flat periodically, but the thoughts of suicide wouldn't leave my mind. I had managed to stockpile paracetamol from the hospital and I was on my laptop looking at what 60 paracetamols would do, whether I needed to get more, or different, tablets.

Once I had done what I needed to do, I went into my browser history to delete it in case Rob used my laptop and saw what I had been up to. In the search history there was 'xhamster'. And further down there was 'barely legal' and other pages along those lines. I lost the plot and asked him about it. He admitted to the porn but said that some specific things he had clicked on by accident.

We had a screaming row. I couldn't take any more of this. I couldn't take any more lies and to be left constantly questioning whether people were telling the truth or not. He lost his temper and stormed around my flat, punching walls and shouting at me, asking why I didn't trust to him. To which I screamed, 'because everyone was lying to me and giving me shit from every angle!' I shouted that I'd stuck with him through all this shit and that not many people would have. He started crying and put his stuff in bin liners; he said that he didn't want to go but that it was best for me and that I deserved better.

In the end, he didn't leave. I sat exhausted for a while. Then I started getting wound up. My mum phoned and I got a bit hysterical. She told me to put Rob on the phone and she told him to take me back to the hospital. The whole way back I just cried and sobbed while people stared at me.

That week I got the inevitable news that my job was no longer there for me to go back to. I was devastated that I hadn't been able to pull myself out of this in time to carry with my 'normal' life. It felt like the walls were closing around me.

Rob's trial finally came around. I was pacing up and down. I didn't know what to do with myself. I announced to the staff that I was going to the town centre. They advised me not to, but I didn't care. I couldn't just sit here with people looking in my direction waiting for the phone to ring.

I was in the shopping centre toilets when the phone rang. It was Rob's Dad. He was upset, and I knew what was coming. Rob had been sentenced to a 12 month custodial sentence for incitement of a minor and would probably have to do 4 months. My world crumbled. I sat on that toilet seat and cried and cried until I couldn't cry anymore.

Loud Silence

I found out that on the male ward downstairs people were having drugs thrown over the back fence. I had befriended a couple of male patients and one day I went onto the ward to find out about how to get some cocaine. I paid them, and before I knew it, I was up in the toilets attempting to drown my sorrows by snorting lines off the toilet seat.

One of the girls on my ward, who had done a lot of it herself, suspected what I was up to and so I told her I had some and I gave her a line. She went into panic mode and ended up with the staff. I was furious. I sat in my room for the rest of the evening getting high, luckily no one came in to see me.

The next day it all came out and I was told that I was lucky to be allowed to stay. Dad found out, but at this point I didn't care. Then my mum texted me to warn me that my nan knew. Now that I did care about. My step mum had apparently texted her saying that I was 'on drugs' - even though she had promised that she would keep my affairs private and that she didn't speak to my nan much anyway. The only person that could have told her was dad; so, it was passed down the grapevine and my poor nan was gutted.

I texted my dad to say thank you very much, nan was devastated. He told me that that was a ridiculous thing to say because she'd been devastated for years because of me. He denied telling my step mum and when I argued that he was the only person that knew he simply replied, 'oh well!'

I was so frustrated and fed up of feeling like people were just trying to involve themselves in drama. I barely had anything to do with my step mum now and so there was no need for her to be getting involved. She told me that she was fed up with all of the he said, she said stuff. I replied angrily, saying that she seemed quite happy not to be involved anyway, so maybe it should just stay that way. I just wanted as little interference as possible, and I wasn't up for the added confrontation.

I was in a state. I spent most of my time curled up in a ball shaking, with a tight chest. I felt like I couldn't trust anyone. Regardless of what Rob had done, I missed him terribly as well.

I got a visiting order and went to see him at the prison. I had never been to a prison before and I was terrified. It was a 30-minute process to even get into the building after queuing, searches, passing through one locked door to another, and sniffer dogs. I couldn't believe I was there to see the person that I had loved for so long, that I was engaged to. and had shared a home with for all these years. I was blind to what had actually happened and how little he supported me at the time because to me he was the thing keeping me together, the one thing that I could be myself with - and now he was gone.

When I and Rob's parents had gotten through all the security, we were told to sit at a table for a non-contact visit. I was only allowed a short hug at the beginning of the visit and then no more contact. I was totally heartbroken.

When we first sat down, he wouldn't make eye contact with me at all and he looked like a shell of who he once was. It was incredibly sad for me to see.

I looked around and remember thinking it was like something out of a film. The men were all big and bulky with tattooed faces. Rob urged me to stop looking at everyone. I wondered how he would survive in there.

He went on to tell me that for the first two days he was there he had been in such a state that they had wanted to put him in a padded cell, on suicide watch. I felt my heart break from knowing someone I loved felt that way. I knew how it was to feel that way; I couldn't bear the thought of anyone else feeling that way.

He told me that he wouldn't come out of his cell because he was getting called a 'paedo' and 'nonce' and getting spat at. He also said that men were coming onto him because he looked so young, and it was so bad that he couldn't even have a shower. He was broken. I was broken. I just wanted to get him out of there, but there was nothing I could do, and that tore me apart.

My diaries end here. They end because it was the lowest ebb of my whole life. The anorexia, the self-harm, everything that had happened all joined forces and came at me in one huge shit storm. My brain literally gave up on me. It couldn't cope. I was trying to live, but I couldn't function. I didn't know what I was doing half of the time. My legs were covered in self-harm cuts. One day I was in a particularly bad place. I snuck out of the hospital and went to the town centre, a 10-minute walk away, to buy as many packets of paracetamol from as many shops as I could.

I walked back into the hospital without anyone realising that I had gone – or they didn't give a damn that I had gone. I waltzed back in with no bag check, no questions. I went to my room and stuffed the paracetamol under my clothes in the wardrobe.

My mind was completely preoccupied by suicide. I couldn't bear to be a part of this world anymore. My anxiety was through the roof, and my head was spinning. I walked into the bathroom, snapped the blade out of my razor (I shouldn't have had that either) and self-harmed deeper than I ever had before. I had always cut superficially to prevent bringing attention to what I was doing, but this time I didn't care. I watched the blood pour out of my leg.

My friend on the ward started knocking on the bathroom door, asking if I was okay. I told her that I was fine and to leave me alone. But she wouldn't; she said that I needed to let her in or she was going to go and get someone. I pulled my jeans back up over a wad of tissue, hoping that it would do the trick for a few minutes while I got her to leave. It didn't. I opened the door. She looked down. I looked down to the blood seeping through my jeans and fell onto the bed in a flood of tears. She asked to see the cuts, which I was not happy about, but I decided that I had already lost my dignity. She helped me clean it up and pressed on the wound – I will never forget that moment of kindness when most people would have run a mile away.

She told a nurse that it needed looking at. A while later the nurse opened my door and looked at all the bloodied tissues and jeans. She tutted and threw a wad of bandage and tape my way. She then turned around and walked out. My friend and I dealt with my leg and bandaged it up. I'm pretty sure it could have done with being looked at. It took some time to heal and is still the most visible scar on my leg. One day my daughter pointed to it asked me what it was. That threw me off guard and made me feel terrible. I told her something non-related and she toddled off on her merry way, but I am aware that it will one day have to be explained honestly.

My treatment by the nurse that evening was yet another notch on my poor-NHS mental-health-care, and it hit me hard. It wasn't just the self-harm that went totally ignored, but also why I had done it. Most of the time the nurses, with a couple of exceptions, were only interested in watching television or reading the newspapers in the lounge area, things like this seemed to be no more than an inconvenience.

I was discharged from hospital. Looking back, I have no idea why. I was an absolute mess. I get angry thinking about how they should have seen through the front. Part of me thinks that they just had no idea what to do with me. I was broken. A lost cause. There was no way through this, and they could see it. I was given no diagnosis, no real plan, and before I knew it I was back at an empty flat. No noise buzzing from the ward, no staff, no friends, no job, no Rob... just me, on my own. That silence was loud. It was the loudest thing I had ever heard.

I continued to see Rob on my own. He was moved to a prison further away, which meant that I had to get the train to go see him. I enjoyed those journeys. I enjoyed them because I knew that I was going to see him, and because I could just stare out of the window and disappear into myself.

I was losing weight quite rapidly. That anorexic voice had come back to prey on me. I was literally walking around in a daze and the days were disappearing before I'd even realised that they had happened. I was losing myself to my mind.

My dad continued with the texts, telling me how stupid I was for carrying on with Rob. One day, I decided that enough was enough and that I simply could not have this man in my life. It was one of the hardest decisions I have ever made. It broke my heart to finally decide that I would no longer have anything to do with him. I could feel myself losing my mind and I couldn't bear it anymore. I needed to try and save my sanity.

Each visit to the prison had broken my heart more. Rob commented on my weight loss, but neither of us had the energy to make anything of it. It simply was what it was.

Somewhere amidst the chaos at this time, my mum introduced me to one of her friends, who had a son called Nick. I was instantly drawn to him. I always had a bit of a thing for bad boys and he had that about him. I listened to him and his mum talk about how he used to go shoplifting; they talked about it like he had a talent.

We swapped numbers and met up a few times. He spent a lot of time telling me that I should split up with Rob, that I was too good for him and he didn't deserve me. He was aware that I liked him. But I was loyal to Rob, and I always knocked him back. Except for one kiss. Even though, deep down, I did consider finishing it with Rob for Nick, I loved Rob and something told me there was more to Nick than met the eye. I knew that he'd had a problem with drugs. I knew he did coke, but considering my own record, that didn't bother me. Still, I had a feeling there was something else.

One morning, around 2.00 am, Nick called me and I answered. I was going through a period of what I would now consider to be mania and I was barely sleeping at all. I was just existing in this bubble of endless time bouncing around aimlessly from one thing to the next. Nick asked me to meet him. As a totally rational thing to do at 2.00 am, I put on some clothes and make up and walked up the alley in the pitch black to the hospital car park where he had said he would pick me up.

We drove around for a while and then went back to his house and upstairs to his bedroom. I could hear his mum – my mum's friend – in her bedroom next door as he pulled out a sealy bag, foil and other drug paraphernalia. I watched as he took heroin, or 'chased the dragon' as it is known. I immediately felt uncomfortable. I asked if he had any coke, to which he said he didn't but to 'try some of this instead.'

In that moment, the world slowed down. I looked at the foil and I looked at him. I thought about how desperately I wanted everything to go away and how this could be the answer. What did it matter at this point if I became addicted to heroin? I was a mess, my mind was a mess, and my body was still a mess after the withdrawal of the prescription drugs. I just needed it all to stop.

He told me that it was fine. It wasn't what people thought. You wouldn't get addicted if you just had a little bit. I watched as he did more and closed his eyes. I watched him almost go into a trance, like falling asleep, and I watched his muscles occasionally jerk.

I can't tell you how close I was that evening to doing heroin. I have an addictive nature and in that one moment my life could have so easily taken a whole new path. In my mind, my hand was reaching for it. It took all of the sense I had left not to recreate the picture that was playing out in my head.

Luckily, my brain had enough sense in that moment to tell me no. I looked at him and thought that no matter how screwed up my life was, if I did this it could be the final straw. It would be something that I might not be able to come back from. Deep down I still had a longing to live my life. I wanted to be like all the other people I walked past on the street. I looked at them and thought about how nice it would be to just be walking down the street. I wanted normality. I still had a small shred of hope that maybe that could be possible - and this wasn't the way to go about it.

While Nick was out of it, escaping whatever it was that he couldn't face, I got up and left. I walked home, and I never saw him again.

I spent a lot of time at Rob's house with his parents because I couldn't bear to be on my own. I didn't know what I was supposed to be doing. I am still forever grateful to them. They pretty much took me in and looked after me. They were there when no one else was and I often wished that they were my parents. I wished my mum and dad would be there for me as much as his were.

They saved me. Without them there, without having their house for me to go to, to have that bed to sleep in and to have those meals cooked for me, I don't know what I would have done. I'm pretty sure I wouldn't be here now.

The time had come. I'd had enough. I couldn't think. I wasn't functioning; the only way out seemed to be death. I couldn't see anything else. My brain was broken. I remember sending a message to a friend, and it didn't even make sense. I had made my decision and I was fairly at peace with it. It was like a calm wave had come over me. I didn't need to fight it anymore. This was the end.

As I wrote letters to the people that mattered, I barely shed a tear. This was for the best and it was the way it had to be.

I had enough tablets – old antidepressants, lorazepam, mood stabilizers, and regular painkillers – and I sat on the floor in my lounge, on my laptop, looking at everyone's Facebook lives, just taking pills one after the next.

It's a time that is very hard to explain. It was like I couldn't remember what I was doing from minute to minute. I would do something, but then wonder if I had really done it. I was writing down what I had taken to keep track, to make sure that I had taken enough without forgetting.

There was no going back. This is what I wanted. I could no longer live like this. I couldn't put people through it anymore. I had tried; I had fought; it wasn't getting any better. I had thought that if I beat the anorexia, it would all be okay, but it wasn't. I wasn't supposed to be here.

All of a sudden, a mutual friend of mine and Rob's, Craig, who had been there for me when Rob was sent down, popped up on Facebook messenger. It was strange, as I had only ever spoken to him on the telephone, never online.

I believe he asked me if I was okay and what I was doing. I don't remember the exact conversation, but I must have admitted what was going on because the next thing I remember was him at my front door. I don't know how long that took and I don't know how many more pills I took, it's literally a blank space. I don't think I had blacked out, but my mind had, and in some ways that's even more terrifying.

I remember nothing about how I got to the hospital. Nothing about the people I saw. Any conversations I had, or anyone whom I may have spoken with. All I remember is lying on the bed at one point, feeling extremely confused, yet still desperately grasping at the pretence that I was fine. It is completely terrifying that the brain can switch off to that extent.

Apparently, I hadn't taken enough to do any lasting or real damage, but I remember nothing - apart from at one point realising that I had run out of cigarettes and being adamant that I was going to get some. I remember people not wanting me to go and telling them I was going anyway. Somehow I was allowed to walk out of the hospital and to take the 15-minute walk to the shop to get some cigarettes. I feel for the person that served me because goodness knows what I looked like, let alone if I even made any sense.

Apparently, I had a meeting with the on call psychiatric team. I told them that I took the tablets because I wasn't sleeping and that I just wanted to sleep. I was convincing them that I was okay and no one needed to worry about me. I don't remember those people, that meeting, or saying any of those things. It seems that even in the depths of despair, totally unaware of what was going on around me, I was still able to convince complete strangers – medical professionals, even – that I was fine and needed no help or intervention. That was how hardwired my brain was at doing this. That scared me for an awfully long-time afterwards, and it still does.

I am still grateful for the message that popped up on Facebook. I really don't know what would have happened if it hadn't, nor do I know what I would have done without the care and kindness Craig gave me. I will never forget, even if we don't see each other often these days. It goes without saying that he saved me. Not just at that time, but for months to come. He was always there. He was someone I could turn to and that I knew had my back. I desperately needed that in my life. I still really believe that in a lot of ways I owe my life to him. I never forget someone's kindness, ever. I will never forget that.

The following weeks passed in a blur. I know that I spent lots of time at Rob's house to avoid being on my own. I remember not sleeping, not functioning, going to visit Rob in prison, and missing my dad.

I was still seeing my doctor at the eating disorder unit. I remember walking around Rob's house in the early hours of the morning with a scrap of paper and a pen. I was crying because I couldn't remember what I had done over the last days, weeks, months. I had no idea. I was sat there trying to write down what I remembered. I didn't know what I'd done, who I'd spoken to, what I'd said. *Nothing*. I knew I was due an appointment with my doctor, but I didn't know if it was upcoming or if I'd already had it. At that moment, Rob's mum came downstairs. She hugged me, and sat with me to try and write down something that resembled a timeline. I was utterly broken, in every sense of the word. Looking back, I desperately needed to be in hospital, but I bypassed the system.

Once again, I sat with a load of tablets in a big bag that I had stockpiled. This time, I knew that I didn't really want to die. I desperately needed help, but I wanted to survive. I just didn't see how it could possibly be done.

As a last-ditch attempt at a scream for help I looked up helplines. I rang the number, sobbing. I told them what I was going to do and that seemingly no one could help me. I wanted to hear words that would save me. I wanted someone to tell me something that would make everything click into place. Instead, I found myself frustrated by something they said. I don't even remember what it was. For me, that was it. I put the phone down.

I turned my phone over so I wouldn't see any calls or messages, and I thought about what I had to do.

They must have tried to call back and left a voice message, but I didn't see it. The next thing I knew there was a hammering on my door. I looked out of the window and saw two police cars and a police van. I panicked. Then there was a voice booming through my door telling me that I needed to let them in or they were going to force entry. Absolutely petrified, I let them in.

There were a number of police officers and police vehicles outside, all for me? They had been alerted by the helpline after my phone call and lack of response. The tablets were taken from me and I was told that I had to go to the hospital with them.

I felt like a criminal as I was marched to the police car. Arriving at the hospital, I was taken through the main Accident and Emergency, or A&E, entrance with a police officer on each arm and everyone staring at me. I was terrified and felt like I'd done something wrong, not that I had just wanted to end my life.

The police officer placed the bag of pills on the desk and explained in a loud voice, with everyone looking, what had happened. I was distraught, hugely embarrassed, and totally ashamed. As soon as they let go of my arms, I ran off. I ran as fast as I could. I made it out of the hospital, through the main entrance, and down the path outside before I police officer caught up with me. He grabbed me like a criminal on the run and told me I needed to calm down and go back inside or I would be arrested and spend the night in a cell.

Based on this experience, I have since done an interview for BBC News about the use of police officers and cells in the treatment of mental health conditions as part of MIND, one of the biggest UK charities, which campaigns to improve services, raise awareness, and promote understanding of mental illness. This sort of thing desperately needs to become something of the past. It is in no way, shape, or form helpful. People with mental illnesses are not criminals and should not to be made to feel like it. I was desperately vulnerable and the last thing I needed was the heavy-handed approach.

Once again, I was allowed to go. I don't know if I fed them another line or whether they came to see me as an attention seeker, I don't know, but I was free to go back to my own devices once again.

There was a fight in me somewhere; I know there was. It was lost and suffocated, but I know that there was still a small part of me that wanted to live. Part of me that wanted children so badly, wanted to be normal, and thought that maybe, just maybe, it was possible, but it was hard to cling to that when I couldn't even remember what I was doing day to day. There were times I'd eat a full meal because even the anorexic voice forgot it was there. I would speak to my mum on the phone and the second I put the phone down I wondered whether I'd just spoken to her or if I had imagined it. It was terrifying. I believed I would never get my mind back, that I'd lost it forever.

I know now that it had shut down due to the pressure of the preceding years, especially the most recent situations. It simply couldn't cope. It had broken the way any bone would have, with that amount of pressure.

My moods continued to fluctuate wildly. I went from feeling like I was on drugs: walking down the road rhyming everything in my head at superspeed, deciding that the local shop should be made into a place of worship because everyone would flock there and learn the truths of the world. One day, I locked myself out of my flat and out of sheer frustration, rather than waiting for someone to come out to sort it, I grabbed a rock and smashed the glass. The window was double-glazed and had thick wire in the frame. With the rock, my fist, and the sheer force of anger and frustration I completely ripped my hand to shreds. I didn't even feel as the blood dripped off my fingers. I had to borrow money to have it fixed, but it didn't even occur to me at the time what I was doing. God knows what my neighbours thought, no one even came out to see what was going on. Not that I can blame them.

There was one more cry for help with tablets, and, once again, Craig came to the rescue. He and another friend, Chris, stayed with me in the hospital for hours afterwards. I remember that as I lay on the bed, they sat on two chairs by the side of my bed, in the tiny cubicle that I had been put in, with the curtain pulled to try to retain some privacy. In these hours, I managed to laugh as they attempted to lift my spirits. It seems strange that in such a desperate time, I managed to find some hope. They were there for me unconditionally. As I watched them fall asleep on the hospital chairs, I thought about how no one had ever done that for me before. I appreciated that night so much and I still do. It's something I will never forget. I'll never forget the kindness I felt at that moment; I still feel so grateful to them both.

When the ward doctor finally came around, approximately 24 hours later, he was completely uninterested. He looked at me and told me that all I had done was waste people's time and NHS money.

Before he could even finish, I was up, out of that bed, and running out of the hospital. Craig came running after me and Chris stayed put to tell Dr. Phillip Bright (a name that is engrained in both our memories) *exactly* what he thought of him.

I was coaxed back to the hospital and the nurse in charge proceeded to tell the doctor to get the hell off her ward.

We were back to waiting, but now we were also waiting to make a complaint about Dr. Phillip Bright, which we did. The head of department assured us that she would personally deal with him.

Chris and Craig were told that there was a possibility that I would be sectioned. They were waiting for the Rapid Assessment, Interface, and Discharge, or RAID, mental health team to come and assess me. As it turned out, RAID deemed me fit to leave.

I desperately tried to pull myself together. I thought about that period of time after I left the eating disorder unit, where things had been better, or at least there was some hope. That seemed like a million years ago. It was so hard to hold a new thought, let alone what seemed like a distant memory. Surely, I had to be in there somewhere; surely, there was something worth living for. Surely, there was something I could cling to that would make this nightmare go away.

THE SAFETY OF MY HEARTBEAT

For quite some time, I had been taking more lorazepam than my prescribed dose. Almost without noticing I had gone from taking it 'when needed', to taking six or more every day.

I had also been prescribed venlafaxine, a different antidepressant, by my community psychiatrist.

No one knew that I had been taking that much lorazepam. I hadn't thought for one second that I was addicted to them. I was taking them to get by. Yes, if I forgot to take them, I felt physically sick, but it didn't occur to me that I had an addiction. I wasn't aware of much at that time, let alone something like that. From my perspective, I was simply doing what I needed to do to survive.

After my last hospital stay and my growing record with tablets, the doctors deemed it necessary to stop all of my medications. I was allowed nothing. I went through a terrible period of withdrawal. I would get an electric shock in my head and visibly twitch. I would sweat, especially at night, waking up soaking wet. At times, I couldn't even hold a glass without it nearly being thrown from my hands because of the twitches and shakes.

I was still unsure what was going on a lot of the time. However, with the support of my friends, I managed to get through it, hour by hour, hanging on by my fingernails. In particular, Chris and Craig, along with a few other mutual friends, would come to see me. One bought films to distract me, and he still comes with a film every Friday.

They sorted out my flat, which was a mess. I hadn't slept in my bed since Rob had gone to prison. I couldn't face it. I had no money coming in at all. I didn't have money to buy cigarettes. I didn't even have money to buy food, not that I had been eating. They helped me in any way they could. They went through my fridge and cleared out the various mouldy items, including milk from weeks earlier and God knows what else.

I cried when I found out that they'd done this. I was so devastated by the state of everything. I simply hadn't noticed it while walking around like a zombie.

Chris was becoming more of a regular figure in my life. He saw my pain and my cries for any medication that would stop the horrendous withdrawals. We went to the hospital together to talk to someone who we hoped could help me. I was called into a room of people. They looked at me in a way that I will never forget. It was the same look people give to an abandoned puppy that they can do nothing for.

One nurse asked me how I'd been doing since I last saw him. I looked at him blankly; I had never seen this man before in my life! He looked astounded and explained that he'd been there – along with some of the other people in the room – the evening that I'd taken all those tablets. He told me that I had said that I'd taken the tablets because I wanted to sleep. He said, 'you do remember that?' I told him no, I didn't remember that. I didn't remember the meeting, I didn't remember saying that, and I had no idea who he was. His eyes went slightly wide as he looked at his co-workers.

I went on, begging and crying. I tried to explain the withdrawal I was experiencing and that I *needed* some lorazepam, just to take the edge off. I saw the nurse look away with tears in his eyes. Another staff member explained that they were so sorry but there was nothing they could do; they had been instructed that under no circumstances was I to be given any tablets. I have since been told that this shouldn't have happened. They should have weaned me off the medication because sudden withdrawal like that is dangerous.

There was nothing I could do but battle on and pray it would end. I still wanted to die a lot of the time, but I clung to the ray of hope that these new-found friends had brought into my life. They included me in their meetups. I went to their houses and I spent a lot more time with Chris. He had a calming effect on me. He would talk to me in a way that I understood, and that gave me some hope.

He stayed on my sofa a lot and would make the journey to work from my house. Even though I would be awake through the night, walking from room to room, having him there was enough to stop me from acting on any of the thoughts that still plagued my mind. I was so unbelievably grateful. Having these friends around me made me stop thinking about not having my dad around as much and Rob.

They also helped to clear some space in my head, so I could think about Rob and what was going on with him. I had still been going to visit him religiously, but as the withdrawals started to subside and I could cling to more than one thought at a time, I started thinking about the situation.

Rob's mum and dad asked me whether there was anything going on between Chris and me. I answered honestly that there was not. I hadn't looked at him in that way once, not for a second. I didn't have the brain space. I just felt very lucky to have a good friend that was looking after me.

I had been tormenting myself about Rob's prison sentence. Had my mental illness pushed him too far? What really happened? It didn't make sense to me that the girl would have said to him, 'you have to take my number and text me because if you don't, I will go to the police and say you have tried to rape me.' Anyone in their right mind would have just said, 'go on then,' knowing that there was nothing to hide.

One day Rob's mum handed me a piece of paper and said, 'I thought you might want to see this.' It was a sentencing report that had been stuffed in to Rob's dressing gown pocket. I read it and it made sense. It's funny how a couple of words can change the whole outlook and reasoning of something.

What she had actually said, was that he needed to *carry on* texting her, or else she would go to the police and say that he had tried to rape her. That made all the difference. He had already been texting her. I also saw some of the texts between them. Thanks to my amazing ability to block things out, I don't remember what they said. I just remember that I was shocked by some of them. I wasn't expecting that; it really hit home.

One day, I was looking out my flat window and thinking it about it all. My visits to Rob had dwindled. It was obvious that I had been misled. I had stood by him all this time, but if I had seen that report from the get-go, I probably wouldn't have. I stood, looking at the clouds and the people walking past. All of a sudden, it was like something came over me. The thought was loud and clear: 'what the hell am I doing?' I couldn't be with Rob. It broke my heart, but it was over.

Did I think Rob was a paedophile? Absolutely not. That's not just my misguided brain – everyone has said the same thing. I think he made some really stupid decisions and got caught up in a situation that he couldn't get himself back out of. Whatever the circumstances, I was devastated that my six-year relationship had come to this. Regardless, there was no going back from it. In a way, it was like a weight had been lifted from my shoulders.

I started spending more time at Chris' house. There was nothing going on between us, I just felt safe there. He'd go to work and I'd stay in his flat with a calm feeling that maybe, just maybe, it was all going to be alright.

This doesn't mean it was plain sailing. I had another few dramatic dips in mood and another 'fizzy brain' episode. While he was at work, I went around cleaning his flat, talking to myself. One day, I became convinced that there was evil trying to find me at his flat, the red lights on the stereo were a sign. I became obsessed with anything red being a message from God, I just had to work out what it was. I remember being agitated because I couldn't figure it out. The air wasn't clear enough. While the air settled enough for me to be able to work out what I needed, I decided to gather as many red objects as I could find and store them in a box under the bed.

Once again, this episode ended with a suicidal depression that I had to drag myself out of.

Anorexia was back in my life. It crept in without any awareness on my part. I was thin again, I wasn't eating, and I was making myself sick. I was still cutting frequently. However, I was remembering what was going on more and I clung to that tiny piece of hope with both hands.

That period of my life still terrifies me. I found it very hard to speak about it, or to find a way to explain it. I have a three-month period that is a big black hole. I have a few snapshots of events that I can piece together to resemble something of a timeline, but there are massive chunks of time that I have no recollection of. The fact that I managed to have the meeting at the hospital and not even know I was there, but still managed to convince them all I was fine, is incredible.

It is terrifying that a mind can shut down like that. It's definitely one of the periods of my life that bothers me the most. I get a very strange feeling when I think about it

It was clear to me that my moods weren't normal. I had been looking on the internet and came across bipolar disorder. As I read the symptoms, I almost felt sick; I realised that I was reading about myself.

There was no way I could talk about it to the psychiatrist I had been seeing. He had no interest in me whatsoever. Each visit he asked me what I had been doing and what my plans for the future were. He showed no concern or interest in the previous situations, and I wonder to this day whether he had a disliking for me or if he hated his job. I spoke to someone in recent years who had been under his 'care' who had had similar dealings with him, so I'm inclined to lean towards the latter option.

I started looking into private assessments. I found one specialist who was quite a ways away, but seemed to have a very good reputation in diagnosing mood disorders. I contacted the clinic and was told that her assessments were approximately three-hours long and that I should bring any school reports or mood diaries with me.

Between Chris and I, we got the money together. I gathered as much information as I could and in September of 2010, we made the journey.

It was an extremely long and intense assessment. I filled out a lot of questionnaires, she looked at my school reports and diaries, and I was totally honest about all of the bizarre moods I'd had, despite feeling incredibly uncomfortable. She also spoke to Chris for an hour without me in the room. Halfway through, she took my diaries and reports and said that she was going to take a break to go through them all. We waited in the grand building and I remember looking around thinking that I bet the patients in this hospital didn't get spoken to in the ways I had been.

She was incredibly understanding and listened to absolutely everything I said. At the end of the four hours she told me that I had bipolar disorder with rapid cycling, meaning that the mood cycles did not follow a particular pattern and that I'd had a recent manic episode with psychotic features.

It had been insinuated previously that I had a personality disorder and I had told her this. She said that I had had a traumatic past, which meant there would be some personality traits that led to less functional ways of coping. However, she did not believe that that was the reason for my moods, nor that I had a diagnosable personality disorder.

When she said those words, I cried. I cried because I was relieved. I cried because I was scared. I cried because I thought there was stigma attached to bipolar. I cried for my fight to get this diagnosis. I cried because I couldn't believe this incredible woman was being so kind to me.

She sent me a six-page report which stated the complete diagnosis:

- Bipolar disorder, rapid cycling, with a recent manic episode, with psychotic features.
- Anorexia nervosa, with an underweight BMI of currently 15.5 – advised to start outpatient treatment.
- Difficult upbringing – personality traits resulting in dysfunctional coping mechanisms, but I believe these are exacerbated due to the fact that she has bipolar disorder and becomes very distressed when high and irritable. I do not believe that she has a personality disorder.

She made her recommendation for an antipsychotic medication. I clung to this report. This was my lifeline. No one could dispute this. I was finally going to get some help. It was finally going to start getting better. I had such a huge wave of hope that I cried again.

I had no choice but to take this to the dreaded local psychiatrist. I was so nervous because of how he conducted himself, but I had hope. Maybe he'd see that he had been missing something.

I handed him the report and I instantly knew that it had trod on his toes. He didn't read it, he simply flicked through the pages, barely looking at it. He then told me that my problem was that my life was 'boring, empty and pointless.' I was gob smacked. I literally had no words. I felt like it was my dad's voice coming out of his mouth. I cried and told him about the recent episodes, that surely he was mistaken. He disappeared out of the room and came back with a prescription, which he thrust in my direction with total disinterest, and I left.

I broke down into a million pieces. He must be right. All these doctors must be right. They are doctors! It must just be me. I must just ooze someone that is making it all up. I cried until I was exhausted and all of the hope from that private appointment evaporated.

Chris was fuming. He phoned and demanded an appointment with the doctor. We went together and when we walked in the doctor looked uncomfortable. Chris did nothing more than tell him that he wanted to know how he thought telling a vulnerable patient at a time in her life that had been pretty horrific that her life was 'boring, empty, and pointless' was helpful. The psychiatrist looked everywhere except at us. He didn't know what to do with himself. He stood up and walked out of the room saying that he didn't want to talk about it. The poor student who was also in the room at the time stood there with her mouth open. He refused to come back in; we stood up and left.

After that appointment, I refused to see anyone regarding my mental health again. I couldn't bear it anymore. It was easier to live with no help than to try to get it.

Over the following months, I very slowly put myself back together. I tried to build on one day at a time, but it was all still quite a blur. Anorexia was back in my mind, but the thoughts just hung around in a daze. I didn't really fight or not fight, it was just there lingering in the background and I went along with whatever.

Chris and I started getting closer; we'd hug on the sofa, it seemed natural, but there was still nothing more between us. I booked tickets for us to go see Alicia Keys in concert. There was one song that really resonated with me; he knew which one it was, and when it came on, he held my hand. My heart, for the first time in a long time, felt happy and safe.

Walking home from the concert, I held his hand. I hadn't been thinking about him in this way up until this point – or at least I didn't think I had – but in that moment it just felt right. That night was the first time we kissed. I was unsure if it was the right thing to do. I still had Rob in prison, even though I think we both knew, deep down, that it was over. However, I still had Rob's mum and dad in my head. They had looked after me more than anyone else through these times and they had already asked me if there was anything going on with Chris. At the time there genuinely hadn't been, but maybe they sensed it before we did. Either way, I felt like I was betraying them. Still, I couldn't deny that I felt something for this man. I felt safe around him, safer than I had felt in a long time.

Chris and the group kept me going. No one knew about Chris and me. We decided that it wasn't a good idea to make anything public; it was all still very new.

Six months passed in a blur and Rob was due to be released from prison. I thought back to when he had first been sent down; I had imagined meeting him at the prison gates with a huge embrace, being so happy that he was finally home. Things were very different now. I just texted him. We hadn't officially split up, we hadn't said the words, but we both knew it. Craig and Chris went for a drive while Rob came to my flat. They said they would be back to pick me up after he left.

It felt surreal when he stepped back into my flat. He barely looked at me and not much was said. He told me that he had come to get his stuff and he gave me back his key. I remember watching him leave with tears pouring down my cheeks. They were tears for everything that had happened and everything that had been lost.

I rang Chris and they came to get me. I got in the car and as we talked and played music, things felt just a bit better. I knew it was for the best, but it was hard. I still felt a bit confused about my relationship with

Chris. In fact, in that moment of clarity that I'd had looking out my window that day, I had sworn that I needed some time on my own, time to live with myself. I worried that I was jumping into another relationship for the wrong reasons. Especially because it was not just any relationship, it was with one of Rob's very good friends. Still, it wasn't something either of us had planned.

My flat was on a popular path to the town centre, train station and bus stops. Rob's house was within walking distance, so I frequently saw him walk past, or I would walk past him. We would often cross the road so as to not have to walk directly past one another. I couldn't take it. Although I spent most of my time at Chris' house, I decided that I needed to move.

My flat was in a great location, and with technology these days, I'm sure I could have had my pick of council house exchange. Back then, it wasn't so easy and I ended up with a less desirable exchange, to an area that I wasn't very familiar with. The girl I exchanged with probably thought all her Christmases had come at once. To this day I regret that move – I was so lucky to get that flat. However, at the time, for my sanity, it was necessary. The new flat was tiny and not in a great area, but it was okay, and I was happy to be moving on.

It came out that Chris and I were in a relationship. Chris lost some friends because people didn't agree with us being together. Others were fine with it and said that it had been obvious anyway.

We were very happy together. We had known each other since I was 16. I had been around his flat for parties and been friends with his ex-girlfriends. Somehow it had happened, we were not strangers, and it felt natural, like we had been together for a much longer time.

While Rob was in prison, I had bought a dog. I was hoping that it might give me a focus. It was something to look after, to occupy my mind and to make me leave the house to walk it. I adored him from the moment that my little Chihuahua and Yorkshire Terrier mix, or Chorkie, Alfie, came into my life. I loved him with all of my heart. I still remember the day I got him, walking him around my flat, showing him the rooms and telling him I would look after him for the rest of his life. This tiny little bundle of fur used to sleep on my neck on the sofa. While I was terrified to sleep in my own bed, he would fall asleep to the safety of my heartbeat, and I would fall asleep so thankful for this little thing that was saving me from myself.

After a while, as I was spending all my time at Chris' house anyway, and he was getting some threats in the aftermath of Rob, we decided that it would be best for him to move in with me. It made sense, and it felt right. So, it was Chris, Alfie, and me after that.

IT WAS A GIRL

The move was what I needed. I felt like I was far enough away from Rob for the memories to lie dormant. I was also no longer in eye view of the hospital where I had spent so much time.

I had still been seeing my doctor from the eating disorder unit, even though it was technically not his job, because I should have been purely under general psychiatric care. Still, he made time for me, sometimes after I was sure that he should have already left for the day. He never rushed me, never made me feel anything but safe, because he was there if I needed him. I will *never* forget this psychiatrist's kindness towards me. He remained professional, but he went above and beyond his professional duties on many occasions. He never passed me off, never told me that I couldn't see him anymore. His kindness saved me many times.

I remember one appointment with him when I had a 'fizzy brain' episode. I'm sure it was a hypomanic episode. I had been restless and jittery, moving from one thing to the next without finishing anything at all. I had decided that I was going to write a book about my experiences. I had found a publisher that was all about mental health stories and I was determined that I was going to write mine. Of course, it was completely the wrong time, but I chatted to him excitedly about it. I wrote down the publisher's website to share with anyone else who may want to embark on the process. I told him that I had been diagnosed with bipolar disorder, and he looked at me and nodded. He said that he'd thought that too but it wasn't his place to say.

Very occasionally, after our appointments dwindled, I wrote my doctor letters to tell him what was going on in my life. In one letter I must have mentioned the book again; whilst going through my diaries and writing this book, I found one of his letters thanking me for letting him know how I was getting on and to let him know if my manuscript was published. I smiled and thought how much I will look forward to sending him a copy with a thank you note for saving my life, many times.

After the move, my weight continued to drop. Anorexia had slyly snuck into my life again, without my awareness of it. It had gotten to me again. I saw my doctor, and we agreed that I needed another inpatient stay to get myself back on track. He didn't think that it wouldn't be a long stay. I agreed; I knew that this time was different. Anorexia had gotten me back into the grip of an obsession with control and counting, but my obsession with my weight and the competitive anorexic streak wasn't there. I basically needed a kick up the arse to get me used to eating again. I needed someone to take the reins away from me for a while, so I didn't have to handle breaking that anorexic bond on my own, and deal with all of the guilt attached to that.

I went back to the hospital in a strange mood. I felt restless and agitated. I remember that first snack, sitting at that table once again, but this time I ate the food with much greater ease. I was chatting away about nothing, the other patients were looking at me with 'shut the fuck up' in their eyes, and the nurse was giving me a quizzical look.

I carried on without too much of a problem. It was nothing compared to the previous two admissions. I did have a couple of incidents where I kicked off for one reason or another. Someone had said something in a support group to another patient that I didn't agree with, I thought it was very judgemental. I would have usually sat in silence, but I stood up, told her what I thought, and left the room.

It was a younger group of girls this time and there was a bitchy environment. Considering all that I'd been through prior to this admission, I didn't have the tolerance. I was probably gossiped about; I think they were a little intimidated by me, and I had no desire to make friends, so I kept to myself.

One snack time, shortly after my group outburst, I realised that I was given a drink that I had not put on my sheet. I explained that it was not what I had ordered. I was told that it must be what I'd ordered, and that I needed to 'challenge myself.' I knew I hadn't ordered it. The nurse told me later that what I had actually asked for had been crossed out and written underneath was the drink I currently held. I was fuming! I turned around and said that whoever had done this needed to take a long hard look at themselves and imagine that it was them. I said that luckily I was in a position right now that it didn't really bother me, but that this would have broken me on the previous two admissions. I stood there and necked the drink in one, slammed it on the table, and walked out of the dining room.

After only a couple of weeks, it became even more apparent to me that this wasn't what I needed. I wasn't in the same headspace that I had been in regarding eating. It bothered me, yes. I felt guilty, yes. However, the weight gain itself didn't bother me nearly as much. It was more the obsession itself, which I believed was more down to my moods than anorexia.

I told staff this and that I wanted to leave, but they weren't having it. *Who would believe an anorexic with a low BMI when they suddenly announce that they don't have a problem?* It's almost comical., but still, I was adamant.

I spoke to my doctor. I told him how I felt – that I believed this was 'more mood than food.' He said that if anyone came to him with this, he normally wouldn't even entertain the idea, but that he knew what had been going on for me, the bipolar, and he believed me. He agreed that this admission was worlds apart from the previous two. Because of this, just three weeks after being admitted I was back at home.

I had needed that admission in as much as I needed a kick up the arse. I had needed the switch to click back, and I knew it had happened. Slowly, slowly I ate. I still struggled and battled the usual feelings, but the fight was there; I gained weight, little by little, with sheer willpower.

In the three years that followed, in that tiny little flat, I started to return to normality. I didn't push to find work. I knew I needed time; too much had gone on, and I was so fragile. I needed some time to process.

One day, my dad turned up on my doorstep. My brother, who I was still very close to at the this point, and over whom I had always felt protective, had gone missing. He probably used that as an excuse to knock on my door, knowing that I wouldn't be able to turn him away. I invited him in and made him a cup of tea. He showed me a video of himself on a motorbike ride that he'd done with a group of bikers. He told me that there had been an accident, and that he'd had to be airlifted. I felt the usual guilt wash over me; I was terrible for not knowing this. As he was leaving, I gave him a hug. I had missed his hugs. I told him that if he wanted to come over again, it would be okay, but to please let me know that he was coming first. I thought maybe he'd changed. Maybe, just maybe, I could have the relationship with him that I had been longing for.

As it turned out, he never came in contact again. It was like he'd completed a little mission; I'd fallen for it, and that was all that he wanted. I was angry. Very angry. Angry at him. Angry at myself for letting my guard back down.

I was left fuming. I thought about how he was walking around like butter wouldn't melt in his mouth and I was sat, once again, like a dropped sack of potatoes. It hurt very much and in anger I decided to email his girlfriend to tell her everything that he'd done. I sent it anonymously, but it would have been clear that it was from me. I wanted to hurt him. I wanted her to leave him and for him to be left with nothing, just like I had been. I wanted him to feel a tiny part of what I was feeling.

I also wrote him a letter. I told him what I thought about him and that if he didn't admit to me openly and honestly the things he had done, he wouldn't see me again, and that went for any grandchildren that he may have in the future as well.

In the back of my mind, I have always wondered whether he just is the way he is, or whether he has some sort of mental illness. He denies being the way that he is with such a conviction that I've felt guilty making him out to be a horrible person. *If he was ill, how could I judge that?*

For me, the letter was his last chance. His chance to be honest with me, to make me understand. I never heard back from him; I knew that was the end. The email to his girlfriend seemed to have fallen on deaf ears; they're still together.

I shut it out and carried on. I walked Alfie, enjoyed music and books and went on holiday with Chris. We enjoyed numerous Christmases at the Alton Towers Ball; I got an excuse to buy lovely dresses, and we enjoyed ourselves a lot.

My moods were still up and down. I had periods that almost became unbearable, but they passed. I was seeing no health services at all. I refused to see any one after my previous encounters. I believed that it was better to suffer in silence than to share the suffering and get the responses I had received previously.

I had managed to get some diazepam. I took them sensibly, and they got me by. If I got 'fizzy brain,' I would take a couple extra, but I didn't abuse them like

I had before. They just about managed to get me through without any major disasters.

I started taking part in beauty pageants. They have a terrible stigma attached to them, but they were so good for my confidence. I got to dress up, have my hair done, meet some lovely girls, and travel around the country. Most of the time, my nerves got the better of me; I still lacked confidence severely. However, they helped me build back some of the confidence that I had lost, and they gave me a spark that I thought had died forever. Chris always came with me, wherever they were. He told me how beautiful I was and cheered me on. We always had lovely pageant weekends. In fact, in this three-year period, we had some really lovely times together, and many happy memories were made. Chris and I both look back on that time with fondness. It wasn't perfect, but compared to the previous years, it was a period of calm.

As they say, there's always a calm before the storm. One day, I woke up feeling like I was on a boat. My equilibrium was gone, and I felt sick. I immediately thought: I'm pregnant. I bought a pregnancy test and sure enough, there it was. I was pregnant.

I was so happy. I had always wanted children. I couldn't believe it. Then it hit me - I was also terrified. I worried that it was too soon, so much had happened, and I still wasn't on top of things. Thankfully, that faded into the distance as I thought about the baby I had inside me and how much I was going to love it.

Chris was over the moon as we laughed at the row of pregnancy tests that I had done to make sure. The digital one was telling me that I was just six weeks pregnant. This was going to be a very long pregnancy!

From that first day of feeling sick, it didn't stop. Day after day, I felt sicker and sicker. It wasn't morning sickness, it was all day, every day sickness. I could barely eat anything without being sick. It was horrendous, and as time went on, I started feeling more and more depressed.

One day, I had a terrible pain in my side and I could barely stand up. I was bleeding and I panicked. *Please no. I can't take anything else.* We went to the hospital and when the doctor touched my side I almost jumped through the roof in pain. He told me that I needed to go straight to another hospital that was larger and better equipped; he believed it was an ectopic pregnancy.

I burst into tears and was completely devastated. After a scan; I was told that it was too early to see. I had to go back every week to be scanned and for them to test that the hormone level was rising to indicate that it was indeed a normal pregnancy.

After what felt like an eternity of stress, and talking to my tummy in the shower every morning, willing the beginnings of the little person inside to just keep fighting, we were given the all clear. I was tremendously relieved.

After nearly three years in that tiny flat, we decided that we were going to move again. We made a bad move to an area that was far away from everything I knew. I hated it. To top it off, the place was falling apart. Things kept breaking, showers didn't work, the drainage was coming out of the shower plug. It was awful. We didn't even unpack. We knew we couldn't stay there. We had to borrow money to get out of there and back to a more familiar area.

The new house was lovely. It was just what I needed, and a huge relief. With the stress, lack of rest, and constant sickness, I lost the excitement of being pregnant, and instead wondered what the hell I was doing. *Who was I kidding? How was I supposed to be a good parent? How the hell was I going to cope with the weight gain?*

I was horrendously tired. I would get up in the morning, feel sick, throw up a few times, and then fall back asleep for a few hours, only to wake to a horrible dizziness. It threw me down, day after day. I had just started to get my life back and do things I enjoyed, and now this. I wanted to be a parent - I loved the little baby growing inside me - but I also felt trapped. As terrible as I feel thinking about it, I started feeling resentful. I started doubting whether I wanted a baby at all. The depression started to cloud my mind, and I was often a tearful mess.

With the move, I had missed scans and getting assigned a midwife. This meant that I started getting help later than I should have. I desperately tried to keep my feelings to myself. I felt like a terrible person for feeling the way that I did.

Somewhere along the way, it was picked up that I wasn't coping well and that I needed more support. I was referred to a specialty midwife. I didn't want one. I had gone almost four years with no intervention and I wanted absolutely no psychological input from anyone. I turned up to that first appointment extremely guarded.

Luckily for me, and very thankfully, Sue was a wonderful woman. She made me feel at ease from the start. She judged me with nothing but total kindness. I became so grateful for her and her support. At times, I don't know what I would have done without her reassurances. Chris even had her number and was told that he could phone her at any time.

Sue started to try to convince me to see a psychiatrist. My gut reaction was no, no way, definitely not. However, after a few more sessions with her, we agreed that I would give it a try.

The day that I saw the psychiatrist, Chris came with me. I went in with my guard up as much as it possibly could be. I was expecting the worst. I went in with my daggers drawn, before she even began speaking. I rolled my eyes as we went through the usual family history questions that I had become so tired of answering over the years. She asked about previous episodes and I gave as little information as possible. I felt I could not open up, due to the risk of being shot back down. I couldn't do it. I couldn't tell her about the hypomanic episodes, the words wouldn't leave my mouth. Luckily, Chris jumped in. The psychiatrist thanked Chris for making that clear, because of course, it made a massive difference. To my surprise, she confirmed the bipolar diagnosis that I had previously received. I was also taken aback by how kind she was, and that she was actually listening to me.

She then delivered the blow. She was leaving and I would not be able to see her again; I would be passed over to someone else in the mother and baby unit. I agreed, reluctantly, dreading having to do this yet again. However, I didn't feel that there were many other options.

I continued to see Sue and the new psychiatrist. The new psychiatrist was from the mother and baby unit. He was okay, not quite as warm as the lady who had left, but he was nice enough. He prescribed me a mood-stabiliser; we went through my previous medications and noted that both of the antidepressants I had tried in the past had made me manic. I thought back to my time in the psychiatric ward where I was given the mood-stabilisers and wondered whether they had suspected the same, but it had never been discussed with me.

After about five-months, the sickness started to subside. Once the mood-stabilisers kicked in, I felt a sense of calm in my life that I hadn't experienced for a long time. Things felt clearer, less chaotic, and less jumbled up. I started to look forward to the birth of my baby.

I knew it was a girl. There was absolutely no doubt in my mind. One day, while walking my Alfie, the name Emily Rose popped into my head. I knew that was it. That was to be her name. Luckily, Chris liked it, because I don't think I would have budged very easily.

Sure enough, we booked a private gender scan and it was a girl - my little girl. I was over the moon. I was a big Emeli Sandé fan and we went to one of her concerts while I was pregnant. We both noted the different spelling of Emily and how much we liked it, so my little princess was going to be named Emeli Rose.

My mood continued to dip, and I ended up extremely depressed. I was huge. My bump was way bigger than normal; at six months people would comment that 'I was due to drop.' I would smile and say that actually, that wasn't the case, while I was secretly hating every second of the pregnancy.

I was told that I had polyhydramnios – which is basically a lot more fluid than there should have been. At one scan the nurse called all the other nurses in to come and have a look at the abundance of fluid surrounding the baby.

You read all the time about how pregnancy is so amazing – so special and intimate – and it puts so much pressure on mums to feel a certain way. Unfortunately, I wasn't feeling anything other than a side dolloping of guilt that I wasn't feeling the way that I was supposed to.

We went to see someone at the hospital about the possibility of being induced early. I also had symphysis pubis dysfunction, or SPD, – a problem with the pelvis that can occur during pregnancy – which was very painful. I was so big that I could barely walk. If I sat down with my dinner on the sofa, I had nowhere to put my plate, because my bump reached out to the end of my knees!

We explained my discomfort, my distress, and my depression to this unfamiliar nurse, who was suddenly involved in my pregnancy Sadly, she was completely uninterested. She told me that she'd 'see me at 40 weeks.' I walked out in total despair. I didn't feel like myself anymore, I didn't know who I was, and I felt like I'd lost any identity that I had started to build.

I had remained good friends with a girl I met in my first admission on the eating disorder unit. She had become my best friend. We met up all the time. She still struggled with her anorexia and I helped whenever I could. I would have done anything for this girl; I loved her dearly.

I thought I finally had a friend for life, someone who understood me, and I understood her. If she ever needed any help, I was there in a heartbeat. I really valued her friendship. All of that changed when she found out that I was pregnant. For no apparent reason, she distanced herself from me. Perhaps it came as a shock. Maybe she couldn't cope with the fact that I was in recovery, pregnant, and trying to move on. Her excitement seemed false and she seemed uninterested. It really hurt. I'd wanted to share these moments with my best friend.

Each time I tried to meet up, I would get a message along the lines of, 'we will have to sort something out really soon!' It went on like that and one day I snapped. I told her to forget it. I was pretty nasty to her, but I was deeply hurt. She was still seeing another friend, who also had had an eating disorder, and a new baby, so I saw no reason why my situation should have been any different. I concluded that it must just be me, I was a crappy friend and stupid to have ever convinced myself that I could have a long-lasting, meaningful friendship. I'd obviously done something wrong.

I never saw her again after that. It took a long time for me to get over it. I really had thought the world of her, and she hurt me deeply. She was one of the few people that knew everything about me that there was to know; I had really trusted her.

I started to break. I started to think that I no longer wanted this baby. I no longer wanted to be pregnant. It was such an awfully guilt wracking time and I tried to keep as much of it to myself as possible.

My old endometriosis consultant had become involved in the pregnancy. I was grateful for this because she was a great surgeon and I trusted her. Chris and I had a meeting with her towards the end of the pregnancy and I broke down. I cried that I didn't want the baby; I didn't want to be pregnant; I needed this baby out; I was losing my mind. I sobbed and sobbed. Bless her, not being trained for this kind of situation, she looked quite alarmed. In a flash she had disappeared and suddenly reappeared with my specialist midwife, Sue, who managed to calm me down and explain to her what was going on.

My gynaecologist and Sue decided between them that I needed to be induced. I was told that this pregnancy could not continue under the circumstances and that plans were being made for my induction. I was admitted to hospital. I was given a pessary to induce labour. That was the start of an agonising 48 hours. I had some dreadful midwives who treated me like I was a pain in the arse. I reacted badly to pain relief, which made me incredibly sick, and was eventually given an epidural, which was a welcome relief.

I was violently sick and exhausted. One of the nicer midwives commented that she had never seen anyone so sick. I had no energy left to push in the final stages, but I was told that I needed to keep going. I felt my back give way, and I screamed in agony. I couldn't talk to tell them what was going on because the contractions were non-relenting. I kept getting told to push, but I couldn't because my back and my side felt like they were crumbling into pieces. Tears streamed down my face. I knew something was wrong. Chris was getting frustrated from the exhaustion of the last 48 hours. He grabbed me and told me to just push, for the love of God. I remember laying there, thinking that no one was listening to me. What was going to happen?

Eventually I screamed that I didn't want the baby and just get it the hell out of me. They took notice finally and I was taken to theatre where there did an episiotomy and used forceps for the birth of my daughter.

In those final moments I had lost it. I remember looking down on myself, watching it all happen. I also remember looking to the corner of the room and talking to someone that obviously wasn't there. Whether I spoke in my head or out loud I do not know, but I had almost split from reality.

My daughter was born on the 4th of May 2013. I was so relieved that it was over. They tried to hand her to me, but I shook my head. I couldn't have held her even If I'd wanted to; my arms wouldn't work. I felt utterly broken.

I lost a lot of blood and the doctor did not explain to me what had happened, what was going to happen, or what he was doing, nothing. He stitched me up like he was a mechanic working on a car, without so much as a word. When he finished, he walked off.

Emeli was a very healthy weight. The doctors remarked how big she was, especially given that she was four weeks early. Chris was in tears. With all the commotion, he'd started to think that something was going to happen to both of us.

Emeli was taken into neonatal care because she was so premature. She stayed there for eight days. She was given oxygen and was a little jaundice, but nothing more.

I was in agony. I had pushed my coccyx out of place and I couldn't move. I couldn't stand, sit, nothing. It was awful. I was in a wheelchair for about four days, going down to the neonatal ward to see Emeli. I loved her from the second I saw her, but I found it hard that I wasn't doing all that I felt I should have been.

One day I tried to stand and there was an audible crack. Chris looked at me and I announced that it had come from my back. From then on, I was able to start moving on my own accord. I was so grateful to that crack that I could have cried.

We spoke to Sue and my gynaecologist, who had come to visit me every day, about the doctor that had been at the birth. She told us that she knew exactly who he was, as she had problems with him too. He was a locum doctor from Saudi Arabia. She told us that she could assure us that by the time she had finished he wouldn't be allowed to step foot in that hospital ever again.

Before I was allowed home, I had to wait for RAID to assess whether I could go home or whether I would have to spend time in mother and baby care. We were to be leaving the hospital alone, to be leaving the hospital without our new baby girl, as she needed to be kept in to resolve her jaundice. By this point, all I wanted was to go home. Once again, I managed to convince them that I was fine, that I loved my daughter, and that I was just exhausted. I needed my own home and bed to recover.

As I was discharged, I was given some leaflets by a nurse, including one on contraception. She asked me about my contraceptive plan, because women are very fertile after birth. I explained to her that was the last thing on my mind and that I hadn't given it any thought. I just wanted to go home. She looked at me and asked whether 'someone with my condition should have any more children?' I was gob smacked. If had I not been so exhausted and desperate to go home, I probably would have smacked her in the face.

It was strange arriving home, having had a baby and all the new baby cards, but with no new baby in tow. If I'm honest, I was grateful for that period to rest and try to get my head together.

When we were told that we could collect Emeli from the hospital, we prepared ourselves for the new little arrival in our home. Then, just as Chris was leaving to collect her (I couldn't bear to see that hospital ward again), he received a phone call to say that she had had to be put back under the lamp for her jaundice. We couldn't believe it.

Next thing we knew, they were saying that they wanted me to go back to the unit and stay in one of their rooms for parents with premature babies. This is a pretty standard practice, but it felt like my baby was just being kept from me or that they wanted to check that I was a capable mother - that thought ate away at me. I was adamant that I would not, under any circumstances, be going back to the ward. I'd had a traumatic birth and even the sight of the building made me feel panicky. I could think of nothing worse than being there for a night on my own with a new baby under a watchful eye. It petrified me, and I refused. Eventually Chris made a call to Sue. He said that he was starting to lose his patience, we knew there was no reason for Emeli to be kept in neonatal anymore.

Soon enough, our little princess was home. When she needed her first nappy change, we attempted it in a blind panic. Clothes were thrown everywhere! We were trying to figure out what we were doing, just like any other new parent.

When we undid her nappy, we were horrified to see a big patch of raw, bleeding skin. The midwife came, and she went mad. She was fuming, and got straight on the phone to the hospital, telling them that this was not nappy rash as we had been told. This was a chemical burn, caused by a child being left in their own urine for too long.

The irony hit me. Just hours earlier, they were trying to make me go in to make sure I was going to adequately care for my child. I was distraught. I knew I hadn't been changing her nappies as much as the other parents in the neonatal ward because of my back, so they had been doing this for me. Still, I blamed myself and thought that I was a terrible parent already.

The first six months of Emeli's life were difficult. I loved her, but I felt unattached. I felt like I was going through the motions, just doing what needed to be done.

She was a very hungry baby. At one point, I couldn't even get her dressed because she would cry for food, and 10 minutes later she would want more. It would carry on that way for hours and hours. I felt like I was going insane and tried to dissociate my feelings so that I just went from feed to feed, motion to motion. I realised that I became emotionally unavailable to everyone around me. I started feeling resentful, and I hated myself for it. I had always sworn I would be a certain kind of parent, and I felt like anything but.

We were assigned a health visitor and I remember feeling so much pressure. A wonderful lady named Penny walked in to my life. I clicked with her immediately. I was lucky, because I had heard so many nightmare stories about health visitors, but mine was amazing. She was always there for me, and she has remained my friend to this day. She is another person that came along to whom I will be forever grateful.

I had been taken off the mood-stabilizer that I was on due to potentially dangerous side effects. I had a few meetings at the mother and baby unit with the psychiatrist who changed my medication. I remember that at one appointment I was in tears throughout the whole thing, looking around, wondering if my doctor from the eating disorder unit was anywhere nearby (it was the same hospital, just a different floor). I was struggling terribly, and I felt like the old, familiar feelings of despair and suicidal thinking were building, getting ready to explode.

Things got easier. The medication helped a little, and I started feeling a real bond with Emeli. I loved this little girl more than life itself. Still, I felt like I was going through the motions a lot of the time, but I thought I'd be okay, that it was normal to feel the way I did, and that it would pass. I just had to keep going.

MOOD WAVE

During and after Emeli's birth, I'd suffered from depression. I'd had very little support; I just coasted through, hoping it would get better. When Emeil turned one, I was told by the mother and baby unit that I would be discharged because they only looked after mums until their child was a certain age.

There was nothing I could do. I had made it this far and I was sure the rest would come in time. I had a very strong bond with my little girl and good support from my health visitor, Penny. We would get through this last hurdle together. I carried on with hope that things would turn out fine. Things were better than they had been. We were having some nice family time, which made me feel that things would be fine.

My endometriosis was still causing problems. When we had an upcoming holiday to the Algarve, I went to my doctor's office to ask for norethisterone to delay my period. I was wary of taking it because I had not reacted well to contraceptive pills and hormones in the past, but I was adamant that period wouldn't ruin this holiday and the prospect of swimming. *Big mistake.*

Chris remembers that holiday with horror. I became an absolute bitch. I would argue and create rows over nothing. During the holiday, I was convinced that I no longer wanted to be with him, that we didn't get on, that he was always causing problems, and I just wanted him out of my face. Bless him, he went for long swims alone in the sea just to get away from me. I don't blame him at all; I was vile. I believed everything that I was feeling at the time. It didn't feel hormone induced. I left the holiday talking to my mum about possibly going back on the Council waiting list to get my own place. Looking back, I feel desperately sorry for him. He was totally confused as to what the hell was going on. I just turned in to a mad woman!

When we got home, I stopped taking the tablets and things got slightly better for a short time. I never totally came down from that mood wave, though. It lingered in the air like a bad smell that wouldn't totally dissipate. The tablets seemed to spark a period of mood ups and downs. Everything was unsettled. I would snap at the slightest thing. I would become engrossed in craft projects and just want to be left alone. This was followed by periods of depression, where I, once again, struggled to function.

Chris tried to keep up, take over chores, and look after Emeli, but nothing was good enough for me; nothing he did would please me. I had become, quite frankly, and absolute nightmare, especially to live with.

After my discharge from the mother and baby unit, I was not under any services. We struggled to regain some sort of normality, but it simply wasn't working. This went on for months. We tried to hold on to the positive moments with both hands.

I tried to throw myself into my love of crafts. Christmas of 2014 was approaching, and I started making letters from Santa Claus – it seemed like a good distraction. I was selling them cheap, and I had a lot of interest. Before I knew it, I was overwhelmed with orders, staying up late at night to get them done. I told Chris that is was important to me that all the children had a magical Christmas. *Our Christmas.* My own child's Santa Claus letter faded into the background, as my obsession with completing them took over.

Christmas always has the tendency to make me hypomanic if I'm not careful. I get caught up very easily in the excitement, the lights, the music. The problem is that once Christmas is over, I come down with a crash. These days, I am much more conscious of it

One day, Penny came around and saw me in quite a state. She could see that things were not good. I had been spending days at a time in my bedroom hiding from everything and struggling to get showered and dressed.

The familiar feeling of desperation washed over me. I was having thoughts of stabbing a knife through my wrist. The images were graphic and reoccurring. I started to think that it was only a matter of time before it happened. I was a terrible girlfriend, an even worse mother, and I couldn't bear the thought of going through this fight again. The medication wasn't working, so, in my mind, that meant that this was all on me, and nothing was going to help.

Chris had started a good new job that gave both of us private healthcare. He made some phone calls and found out that this would include private psychiatric treatment. We looked at the nearest Priory Group hospital, and in no time at all, I had an assessment with a consultant psychiatrist.

At the assessment, I told him that I felt suicidal. I told him all the things I had been thinking and he said that he thought I should go inpatient. I was starting to think this cycle was never going to end. I would be that mad person that spends their life in and out of hospitals. I hated what my life had become, but I was driven to get well by the thought of my daughter. I did not want her to grow up without a mum. No matter how much I thought she would be better off without me, there was a nugget of logic telling me that I had been through this enough times to know that those thoughts were my mind playing tricks on me. The doctor gave me hope, saying that he didn't believe my medication was right and that it would be looked at. He asked me if I had ever taken lithium, to which I said that I had not.

Penny was very pleased when she found out that I had gone to Priory. She said that if she had come back in few days and nothing had been sorted out, she would have put me in her car and taken me to A&E. That touched me. It may sound strange, but she was my health visitor and she could have called other people in, she could have just left me to it, but she was going to make that decision by herself to try to help me, and that was greatly appreciated.

I got a call a few days later when a bed had become available. Once again, I packed my things and we made our way there. This time was especially difficult because there was now an innocent, beautiful, one-year old little girl in the mix. My heart broke for her as I thought about my own childhood and prayed that I wasn't going to give her the same.

I spent the first couple of days in my room, lying on my bed, staring into space. Once again, I felt like a fraud, like a waste of time, scared to bother anyone, and scared to go and eat in the dining area (which was very different than the dining area I had been used to: it was very clean, all laid out nicely, and the food was a lot better!).

I was introduced to my therapist, Rebecca, and I liked her instantly. She didn't push me. She came across as very down to earth. There were no false pretences or airs and graces. I like that in people. There was a morning group, as well as mindfulness groups, and drama therapy, which I really took to and felt like I got a lot from.

It took me a while to start eating in the dining room and mix with the other patients, but once I did I clicked with another girl called Sarah. We had a lot in common and would sit in the lounge area to talk and watch films. I was grateful for her and to have someone to share time with. I was upset when she left, but there were a couple of others, a man in for addiction in particular, who I also gelled with, and we spent a lot of time together too.

I started to open up in groups and had regular one to one sessions with Rebecca, who helped me tremendously. She's yet another star I've found along the way.

I had some hard times in there fighting my feelings. I felt like a complete and utter mess that was never going to lead a normal life, but I kept fighting. It had changed before, and it could change again.

The only thing that frustrated me was that nothing was being done about my medication. It had been increased, but I was experiencing horrible side effects, including dizziness and nausea, so it was brought back down. Since then, nothing had been done.

During that admission, it was my therapist, Rebecca, who helped me progress the most. I didn't find the psychiatrist very helpful, and my meetings with him were brief. I didn't understand that much about bipolar disorder, apart from what I had read on the internet, and I really wanted a professional to sit down with me and explain what had been going on all these years. Maybe that could help me feel a little less crazy. He always seemed to avoid any bipolar conversation. He said that he liked to observe people before any diagnosis. This confused me, I had already had two previous diagnoses.

I was starting to think that he did not believe the diagnosis and that upset me. I hadn't gone through all I had gone through to start all over again with someone who had known me only a few weeks.

Rebecca knew I was distressed by this. For me, it was yet another person turning around and saying they didn't believe me. The psychiatrist told me that it didn't matter what the diagnosis is, it was the treatment and getting well that mattered. This infuriated me. To me, it's like saying to someone with a broken leg, 'you have got a broken leg somewhere, but we aren't going to tell you which part of your leg because it's not important, it's the healing that matters.' *How would that person know what to do with their broken leg? How would they know which areas to avoid putting strain on? How they needed to rest it? What exactly they needed to do to make the best possible recovery and to avoid any further injury?* Exactly. Details are important. Diagnosis is important and it's also an important part of recovery to know what you're dealing with. It empowers you to access the right support and know what to do next time. This psychiatrist, however, private clinic or not, did not seem to understand this.

My medication didn't change and I believe that with the help of Rebecca and time – because, as with any mood episode, it will lift eventually on its own – I started to feel better. After four weeks, I went home.

I went home better than I went in, but Chris still says that I wasn't quite 'right.' He says that I was still snappy and not myself. There were still issues in the background, but at least I was not feeling suicidal and I felt like I could function much better.

I had occasional follow-ups with the psychiatrist, but I never felt I could be completely open with him. I continued to see Rebecca for the following year. This woman was a diamond. I loved the fact that she didn't speak to me in a 'therapy voice,' or try to feign interest.

She talked to me as a friend would. I felt like I could tell her anything. In fact, I did. I told her things that I have never told any other professional. I told her things that I told myself I would *never* tell a professional, and that is when you know that you have found someone very special indeed.

She helped me through some very tough times. She listened, and we talked through things that had bothered me for years. She made me feel okay about them, like I wasn't the terrible person I always thought I had been. She helped me to realise that a lot of the times when I thought I'd been in the wrong, actually I wasn't, and that some of the things were other people's responsibility. A lot of the time she just let me have a much-needed rant! She is another person that I am hugely grateful to in my journey.

The year passed by with the usual ups and downs. It wasn't great, but I threw myself into crafts and looking after my beautiful little girl, who was growing up quicker than I liked. I was determined to turn things around. I wanted to be a parent she could be proud of. I was determined to be the parent I wanted to be.

HIDDEN IN THE ROSE

During Christmas 2015, the familiar elevated mood greeted me and shook me by the hand. Unfortunately, once my mum went back home after staying with us for Christmas, the inevitable dip followed. Once again, the flatness enveloped me.

We were starting to see more of a cycle to my mood. Chris noticed it before I did. There are specific months in the year where my mood changes. For example, after the clocks change, I now joke that I am a werewolf in disguise.

New Year 2016 rolled in, and things rolled on as much as ever. With it came the daily routine of looking after a small child. I was starting to craft more and would often get my ideas in the early hours of the morning, just as I was falling asleep. I'd make sure to write them down so as not to forget them the next day.

I had also started to get again what I had learned to be 'hypnagogics'. These had started just before my hospital admission the previous year. They happen in the period between sleep and wake. People experience them in different ways: sometimes hallucinations, feeling paralysed, or hearing music. They are not a mental illness in themselves, but often occur as part of another illness or in periods of stress. For me, they have become a marker of when something is brewing, and I need to slow down. They are always images in my mind and spoken words. The words are usually random, a male voice that sounds like it is right next to my ear. The images are dreamlike but vivid; they are usually black and white and are always disturbing faces or horror movie type scenes that shoot into my mind. It's like that moment where you are falling asleep and you jump, feeling like you've fallen. They always make me jump. At the same time, I know they are not real, and they don't bother me as much as a bad nightmare does. Still, they are upsetting and sometimes happen four or five times before I fall asleep.

I was getting more jittery. I was starting a lot of things without finishing them and forgetting what I was doing, which frustrated me. It built up and up and I started to feel full of adrenaline, like I couldn't do things quick enough.

We had been talking about moving again. Emeli was coming up to nursery school age and we wanted to be in the catchment area of a good school. At the time we lived directly opposite a school that I vowed she would not go to. So, we started looking for a new house to rent. This kicked everything up a gear. I became obsessed with moving. I was constantly looking and booking property viewings all the time. Chris started to get annoyed with me, saying that it didn't need to be done instantly, but I wasn't having any of it.

It didn't help that we had a dog. He is smaller than most cats, chews nothing and loves everyone, but nowhere would accept us. It was going to take a while, but with Emeli's nursery and schooling, it needed to be sorted as soon as possible. On several occasions, we thought we had found somewhere, and then it fell through. For me, it was an emotional roller coaster that was just adding to the already building emotions.

One morning, I stood outside the back door, smoking a cigarette, and it hit me what a beautiful morning it was. The sky was bright; the colours were vivid, and the birds were singing so loudly. I remember thinking how God was looking after me this wonderful morning.

This should have been a huge red flag, given my previous episodes and the fact that I'm not religious, but I didn't think and I didn't care. I didn't dare tell Chris because I knew what he'd think, and I didn't want him to make this wonderful feeling into something that it wasn't.

Mania is a difficult thing. For me, at least some of the times, before it gets frustrating and complicated, it's a very beautiful feeling. Almost pure. Think back to when you last had a drink. You were just a little bit tipsy. You were in control, but everything felt great. Everything made sense and you felt like you could conquer the world and all those worries diminished. That's often what the beginning of mania is like. Now, imagine someone told you that you needed to go home, that you'd had too much to drink, that they were concerned about you, and it was time to get in that taxi. You would probably tell them to get lost. They didn't know what they were talking about. You're tipsy, nothing more! How dare they try and stop you from feeling happy and having a good time.

That's pretty much how it feels. When you know that people will react in this way, it's easier not to say anything at all. *Just look how great you feel! This isn't going anywhere bad right? And people will only start going on if you say anything. So, I'll just enjoy it while it lasts.*

Wrong. It very rarely stays for long - not for me, anyway. It either peaks, dips, and levels out without causing too much disruption, or it peaks, causes huge agitation, anger, and confusion, and then crashes like a sack of potatoes. What goes up, must come down, as they say.

That hazy feeling stayed with me. It melted around me, leaving me in a generally good mood. I was preoccupied with certain projects, but I thought I was just focussed and that it wasn't a big deal.

I bought a few mindfulness books because... well... I was feeling mindful. I was so pleased with my proactive self that I took them to my next therapy session with Rebecca. Telling her about them clearly wouldn't have been enough, she needed to see them in person, because these were really helpful books and maybe other patients may find them useful.

She didn't notice that there was anything up with me. She had no reason to, at this point. I was just in a good mood, slightly more than a good mood, granted, but probably not many people would notice when I'm at this stage. I just talk easier and seem happier, I guess.

Gradually, though, it built. The house obsession was becoming ridiculous, but I couldn't see it. One day I was sat down – my mind was spinning and I felt agitated – when I saw someone walk past the house. Then, I saw a van. All of a sudden, I was suspicious of them. I was sure they were watching the house. A feeling of dread came over me. I thought maybe they were rigging the house with cameras and I needed to be vigilant and keep an eye out for this van.

After that, my memory gets a little blurry and fragmented. My mind had begun to wonder. I started feeling increasingly agitated, and I remember sitting on the floor after throwing all of my craft items off of my desk because it was a mess. Everywhere I turned was a mess, there was so much clutter, and it was aggravating my mind.

I sat on the floor crying as I sorted out the huge pile of crafts, my hands shaking, and sweat creeping up my back as I became a hot, sticky, and frustrated mess. I couldn't sort it out quick enough. *Why were my hands moving so slowly?*

Everything was too much; noises were making me jump, the TV had to be kept low, the lights turned down. Once again, everything around me was in high definition. It was all out of sync and closing in on me.

At my next session with Rebecca, she realised straight away that something was wrong. I couldn't make eye contact with her, it felt uncomfortable. I felt like everyone was judging me, including this wonderful lady, who had shown me nothing but kindness.

As I sat down, my phone rang and the noise was unbearable. I struggled to turn it off and eventually slammed it down on the side. Rebecca told me that she hadn't never seen me like this before and was concerned. I don't remember the ins and out of that meeting, but I remember her saying that she was going to get me an appointment with the psychiatrist.

It continued to escalate. I became more and more ill, frustrated, and angry as time went by. I started to think that people were out to get me – that everyone was plotting against me. I didn't even really trust Chris. He made a comment one day about Emeli, and I became convinced that he was in with everyone else and was now planning to take my daughter away. It was terrifying. I couldn't trust anyone. I was trapped. I didn't know what to do. I felt like I was in some sort of movie, totally on my own, trying to out-run the bad guys. It felt totally real.

I started to think that evil was after me. I felt the devil like an undercurrent and had to do things to keep the evil away. I hung red towels on all the doors and put red things in Emeli's room to keep the 'badness' away. I wouldn't let Chris touch them. One day, I think in his own little way of trying to fight my mind, he insinuated that this was not going to help, and that red was a bad colour. Like that, my mind turned: what had I been thinking? He was totally right! I had got this all wrong ... it all needed to be white. And so, I frantically changed everything to white.

It's clear that my mind was in total disarray. I found some diary entries from this period that I had written on scraps of paper with writing that is just barely legible.

Wednesday 17 February 2016

Everything feels out of sync – nothing matches up.

Changed towels from red to white – purity – colour of God – angel wings – it will all go right again now!!

Everyone keeps asking me questions!!! So many questions!! I can't answer them, I don't know where to start because in between the answers is just letters, numbers, colours, rhymes, good, bad, noise ... White noise? Protective noise?

People need to leave me alone so I can figure out what's going on!

I had an appointment with the psychiatrist who, up until this point, had been okay. He hadn't been the best, but he certainly hadn't been the worst. As I walked into his office, I remember feeling like I wanted to crawl out of my skin. It took all my effort to sit down in the chair. I couldn't look at him. I sat digging my nails in to my hand, fixated by the trees outside the window.

Chris had stayed downstairs, hoping that something would happen here to make it all go away. He asked me questions, but I couldn't answer them. It was like words had failed me; every time someone asked me a question, a million things swam round my mind, just random words, letters, everything but an answer. I tried so hard, but would end up crying and getting frustrated and angry. He didn't seem to understand, and for some reason, my anger was directed at him. He told me that if I was going to be like this then he couldn't help me. All I could think was that he had been turned against me too and that he was in on this plan, evil was surrounding me, and I needed to get out of there.

I ran out of the room, past the receptionist who was calling my name and Chris, to the outside, where I collapsed on to a bench trying not to have a panic attack. Chris ran upstairs to demand what the hell was going on. The psychiatrist simply said that he wouldn't be seeing me anymore and that he needed to contact the crisis team.

To this day, neither of us know what happened. I wasn't violent towards him, I was just a total mess. He had admitting power and had admitted me before. For some reason, this time, he simply disregarded me. I wonder whether my crazy was too much for him; but I doubt very much that he had never experienced that before, so it left us all wondering what the hell just happened - including Rebecca, who was very unhappy with him. For me, it was just another let down from a medical professional who I had trusted and told a lot of private information to.

My thoughts alternated between those of heaven and god, all the new items I could craft, and paranoia. It was exhausting. I was barely sleeping; the hypnagogics were rife and woke me up every time. If I did finally drop off, my sleep was broken, and I'd wake up wide-eyed after an hour or so. I disliked going to bed, because it felt wrong, I had so many things I could be doing without wasting time sleeping.

Undated Entry

Too many thoughts. So many thoughts. I can't think one at a time. They are all one thought.

Was thinking when we move house that I want a rainbow garden! You can get rainbow rose seeds and rainbows are closer to heaven so it will be magical!!!!! I think changing the red sheets to white has helped me think about this better!

Feel like throwing away everything in this house, it's a mess and I can't get it clean!!

There're so many things I want to process but I can't write them down – some of the things I go to write down disappear! I go to answer a question and I manage one word before there's 500,000,000 others!

I can't remember. It's like thoughts are being put in to my head and taken away just as quick.

I've started a million things today and done things in what seems like five minutes but then I realise it's been two hours and I realise that I haven't actually started the things I thought I'd finished. Everything is so out of sync!!!

Undated Entry

I've cut a cross in to my leg to show that I'm following a path I've been shown. I just need to figure it all out.

Nothing is enough! I can't get this house fucking clean!! There's noise everywhere, even in the air – in the fucking wind – I hear everything! I know that God is trying to make it safe and so making sure I can hear everything but I can't cope with it!! I know I need to cope with it or else the bad things will happen! There's no silence anywhere, not even in silence! I have to keep it all to myself as no one would believe me anyway but I can hear it!!

Amazingly, the crisis team had been to see me and deemed that I wasn't a danger to myself. When they came, I was dressed smartly, which seemed to give me big kudos points! They said that they had been told, by the psychiatrist, I assume, that I was suicidal. That infuriated me, because, at this point, I was not, and I had not said that I was to anyone. This only confirmed to my paranoid mind that people were plotting against me. He was now trying to get me locked up in a psychiatric unit. I had to keep fighting this evil.

I denied with conviction that I was not suicidal. Apart from that, I kept my mouth shut and gave nothing away. Even in this state, I had learned to be good at hiding what was going on. I made it quite clear that I needed them out of my house, so they left.

Poor Rebecca, the super star that she was, had to listen to me on the phone. In my mind, she was the only person I could trust. She would phone me all the time, speak to Chris, and I'm sure even phoned me at times that she wasn't working. I am forever thankful to her. She simply listened to me go over the same nonsensical statements, speaking where she thought necessary, even though she probably knew it wouldn't make a difference. She deserves a medal.

I had been making a lot of roses in jars – much like the beauty and the beast rose. They had been popular and at the beginning of this episode, I had been making them in abundance – like some sort of mass production factory line worker.

Undated Entry

A thought flew into my head from nowhere - Adam and Eve and roses! This is why I have had so many orders for my enchanted roses! Why I've been thinking about having a rose garden! It all makes sense now!

The rose protected the fruit tree that gave humans incredible knowledge of good and evil!!!! This is what has been going on in my head! I'm starting to understand what it's all about!

It says the rose was listening and so I've put some roses by my bed which will help.

I've been looking this up to find out some more and found these:

'Mystery glows in the rose – the secret is hidden in the rose.'

'Rose recognised as a higher symbol of unfolding of higher consciousness.'

'Since ancient times the rose had symbolised god at work in whatever situation they appear.'

The next piece of paper is simply the alphabet scrawled out and repeated.

I was also convinced, night after night, that there was a figure in the corner of the room. I would sit up, over and over again, checking whether it was there or not, until I started to sweat. I couldn't rest. I felt like there was a presence constantly watching me. Chris remembers the bother that this caused me better than I do, and says that it really caused me a lot of distress every night.

I still find these thoughts and this time extremely difficult to share. It's almost embarrassing. It's like something you see in the movies, something that people make fun of. I struggle to admit that this was me, that this is part of me. It took me a long time to be able to talk about it without crying or feeling like I wanted the ground to swallow me up, but if I am going to write an honest book, to grab mental health stigma by the balls, I think it's important for me to share these moments too.

Slowly but surely, the agitation grew and the restlessness was unbearable. I was due to see the crisis team again, even though they had been nothing short of useless, but I was crashing. That explosion in my mind was starting to fizzle. It had its bang and was trying to come back down, but then it just rested in a place of pure frustration and uncertainty, like it wasn't quite sure what it was doing.

What goes up must come down.

NIGHTINGALE

My agitation continued to rise, and with it came a deep depression. I desperately searched for answers, trying to make sense of the messages I believed I was receiving. In one of my jars, instead of a rose, I put a faux-bitten apple, with lights and Snow-White figurines. I believed it was a sign. An extract from my scribblings describes my thoughts at this time.

Undated Entry

I can't do this, I don't want to be the one to figure this out anymore. On the tree of good and evil the punishment for eating the forbidden fruit was death. Maybe the most recent light jar I made was a sign, it seems to make so much sense, too much of a coincidence???

All these things that keep happening, they lead somewhere and to something. Maybe it's a sign that I can't keep all this together like I should – maybe I'm supposed to die so that this can be passed to someone else to figure out? Someone that can piece it all together better than I can? I'm not a good mum or partner at the moment anyway and no one understands. I can't even play with my own daughter. I have no space in my brain for any of it. I can't figure it out, I can't make it right and I can't make it stop.

I don't want to be thinking anymore. I don't want to be doing but I don't want to be sitting. I just can't BE. It's like my mind has turned in to a million crawling ants – like in a rotten apple – a rotten fruit off that tree just crawling around and I think it's all just a sign that I'm not supposed to be here.

Maybe the crisis team coming around telling me I was suicidal was a precursor – a curse – an omen. Maybe I should – or shouldn't.

My thoughts aren't my thoughts I am sure they are being put there by a higher force.

Everything everyone says is repeating in my mind. Someone says something and it just repeats. It bounces around my head mixed in with other random words and I just can't make sense of any of it.

My mind was addled and manic. While my mind was spinning, my body was screaming 'stop.' I saw the hospital crisis team and they prescribed me a higher dose of an antipsychotic. I took them reluctantly at first, battling the thought that I was thinking these things for a reason and that bad things would happen if I tried to stop them. I also didn't completely trust the crisis team and secretly wondered whether they were going to poison me. Through a combination of desperation, grabbing on to the tiniest scrap of logic in me, and not really caring at this point whether they poisoned me or not, I took them. They made me feel sick to my stomach and so the dose was decreased slightly, but then things started to slow down.

Chris was at his breaking point. Once, in the middle of all of this, he walked out of the house in just his socks. He walked around the block before going into a shop to buy some tobacco. He sat on the wall outside the local pub smoking a cigarette. He had been pushed to the absolute limit and couldn't take anymore. I knew I was to blame, but I didn't know what the hell to do about it. It was a horrendous time with very little help. He dealt with it all alone, apart from the minor crisis team intervention and the help from Rebecca.

As everything slowed down and the medication kicked in, I came down with the biggest crash of my life. I smacked the floor and broke into a million pieces. I had no idea what had happened to me or where the hell I was supposed to go from there. I just kept having images of myself jumping in front of a train. I felt worthless and like a truly awful mother. I felt like I didn't even deserve the oxygen I was taking up. On the rare occasion that I left the house, I didn't bother looking as I crossed the road. I thought that if I was hit by a car, then at least no one would hate me for suicide. It would just be a tragic accident. I prayed for a car to come speeding around the corner. Luckily, it never did.

I had three words repeating in my head, 'one, two, gone.' These were the steps I could take to walk off a train station platform in front of a train. Then it would all be over.

One night, as Chris and I were watching TV, a Stephen Fry documentary came on: *The secret life of a manic depressive*. I just stared at it, trying to drown out the suicidal thoughts. In the documentary, he was in a meeting with his psychiatrist at the Nightingale Hospital in London. I watched in awe at how the psychiatrist interacted with him. He didn't judge; he seemed to completely understand. I looked up him and the hospital online.

After Chris and I had exhausted any hope of treatment in the local area, he made enquiries and found out that his private medical insurance coverage would, in fact, cover the Nightingale hospital.

I emailed them to ask if it would be possible to of see the same psychiatrist as Stephen Fry. As it turned out, he was on holiday, but my details were passed to another psychiatrist who they believed would be able to help me.

A lady telephoned me. I don't remember everything I said, but I know that I was very upset and expressed that I didn't want to live anymore. She made me an appointment to have an assessment. With that, I abandoned any further contact with the crisis team. I felt that they were being about as useful as a chocolate fireguard. During this time they had been coming over every two days; they asked me if I had been having any suicidal thoughts, and when I told them that I was deeply suicidal and shared my thoughts about the train, they told me 'if it gets any worse or you feel like you are going to act on them then call us.' I couldn't help but think, 'I *am* telling you now.' Other than telling them that I was literally on my way to the train station, I wasn't sure what they wanted.

Another time, when I was in a really bad place, Chris called them (as we'd been told to do) and they told us that there were no available slots and I would have to wait until our next appointment. Chris had to try to hold me and a small child together. It wasn't as if we had loads of friends and family around. *And they wonder why so many people commit suicide.*

We made our way to London for my appointment. The journey passed in a blur. I had lost any hope that this was going to help. It seemed like another fruitless journey that would lead to me having to explain it all over again to yet another person. They would, no doubt, decide that it was my dysfunctional childhood that had created these problems and I would be met with some dead end solution that wasn't going to work.

I was doing this for Emeli and Chris, and, of course, my little fur baby. I had lost myself and I didn't really care what happened. I was embarrassed by the recent goings on that lingered and buzzed in the background of my brain, like a faraway dream that made me feel uncomfortable, even though I couldn't quite grasp it. I was utterly broken. After all these years, I couldn't see any way forward.

We arrived at the hospital, where many stars had been treated. Still, I was convinced that I would see yet another doctor who would just think I was a total moron.

How wrong I was. We met with a lady psychiatrist and I liked the look of her straight away. She didn't look like your typical psychiatrist. She had quite a relaxed 'rock' look about her and she made me feel relaxed from the get go. She didn't ask for the mounds of family history that I was used to sitting for so long giving; she was interested in symptoms. Between Chris and I, we managed to give her the lowdown on the more recent episode and previous years. Straight away, she agreed that I had bipolar disorder. There was no question in her mind. It wasn't questioned that I was crazy, or making it up, or beyond help. She actually acted as though she had seen it a million times before – which she probably had – and that there was nothing to be ashamed of.

She made me feel like I was okay, like I was going to be okay. Through the tears and despair, I dared to feel hope. She advised me to go inpatient. She asked me if I had ever taken lithium, or if anyone had ever offered it to me? She seemed quite surprised when I said that I was still taking carbamazepine and quetiapine, when they clearly weren't working. She said that I should try lithium inpatient, so they could monitor it closely.

I had heard this before. During my admission only 12 months before, almost to the day, I had been asked the same questions and told that my medication wasn't right, but nothing had been done; that doctor had let me down badly. I looked at this psychiatrist and how she was looking at me, and it felt different. I believed her.

On the 9th of March 2016, I summoned every ounce of being that I had left in me and said goodbye to Chris and my beautiful little girl. I managed to get on a train – after staring for a long time at that platform edge – and I made my way London.

FOR A REASON

When I got off the train in London, I walked as quickly as I could away from the platform, fighting the reoccurring images of jumping in front of a train. I stopped outside the hospital building to have a cigarette before going in. The nerves were burning a hole in my stomach. I stood there, thinking about all the celebrities that I knew who had passed through these doors: Amy Winehouse, Frankie from the Saturdays and, of course, Stephen Fry.

I felt another pang of hope. In a way, I was so lucky to be here. The fact that Chris' insurance covered this treatment, and if it was good enough for the celebrities, maybe, just maybe, it was going to be better than my previous experiences, but those experiences were still raw in my mind; I found it hard to believe that this time was going to be any different. I also thought about how some of those stars had gone on to lead troubled lives and even commit suicide. I wondered if there was no hope. I thought there were people that just couldn't be helped, and perhaps I was one of them.

I had a knot the size of the earth in my stomach as I waited for someone to come and collect me. I was shown to my room by a kind nurse who went through my belongings to make sure that I didn't have anything I shouldn't. My room was right at the end of the corridor, around a little corner, and I was glad that I'd been given a room out of the way.

I saw the psychiatrist, who assessed me. Once again, she was just lovely. She went through my family history, and I remember thinking that it wasn't so bad because she hadn't done it the second I had met her at the assessment. I don't know whether this was purposeful, but it was a small thing that made a big difference to me.

As with every admission, time is a little blurry. It's as if my brain shuts down for the first few days. I spent most of my time lying on the bed, staring at nothing. I would have conversations with nurses and then forget that I'd spoken to them. It's strange how this pattern has repeated itself in all of my admissions. Maybe so much brain space and effort is taken up by just holding it together, just functioning, that by the time I get there, I shut down. It's as if someone has pulled the plug out and my brain no longer needs to hold a pretence.

Again, it was some time before I ate in the dining room. The dining area was large – almost like a little restaurant. I couldn't bear the thought of going in there, with all those people, and having to sit on my own… or worse, trying to make conversation with someone.

I had lost weight, quite a lot of weight, but not because of anorexia. With all that was going on, I had simply lost my appetite and forgotten to eat – food just wasn't on my radar. A lovely nurse told me that I could have my food brought to my room. I was taken aback by this. I felt like I was being a burden, but she told me that I didn't need to think that.

After that, my food was brought to me on a tray, with a silver dish over the top. I smiled to myself, thinking how different this was. When I lifted the silver dish, I was gob smacked to see a proper meal. There was meat, properly cooked vegetables, and potatoes – it was lovely! I took a photo and sent it to Chris, saying that he was coming to me for Sunday dinner next time.

It was difficult knowing that my little girl was back in Birmingham, away from me. I fretted that she would wonder where I had gone, but we video called a few times a day, after my initial few days of shutdown.

I felt as if the feeling of wanting to disappear forever would never leave me. The manic episode had traumatised me. As I walked along, a sudden flashback would stop me in my tracks, and I'd burst into tears. I felt like a lost cause. I spent the first week on my own with meals being brought to me, only leaving my room for a cigarette.

The psychiatrist picked up on this and realised that the position of my room wasn't helping. She requested that I be moved to a room further up the hall, nearer to the nurses' station. This was a small thing, but it has stayed with me how she had noticed this and made a change that was in my best interests.

One day, while having a cigarette, I started chatting to another smoker, named Sarah. She was the first person that I had really spoken to properly, and I liked her immediately. We were on different wards, but she quickly took me under her wing and introduced me to other people . I am extremely grateful to her for doing that. That simple act made me feel just a little bit more at ease. We soon became good smoking buddies, and I *really* appreciated her kindness.

It was decided pretty quickly that I should be weaned off the carbamazepine and slowly introduced to lithium. This upset me. There is some stigma attached to lithium, and even I couldn't get it out of my head. Lithium is the oldest psychiatric drug, which means that it must be effective to some degree, but it also brings to mind those old 'lunatic asylums' and 'lithium zombies' – people walking around in a catatonic state. For me, it was something that is given to people who are incredibly mentally ill – the sorts of people you see in films or that are really beyond hope. I thought maybe it was the latter and I was so far beyond hope that I now had to take this drug. I was also terrified of its side effects. I have always been sensitive to medications, not just psychiatric drugs, anything. It can also be a dangerous drug; it is monitored by the level in your blood – too low and it wouldn't do anything, too high and it can be fatal.

I cried when I was given the first Lithium tablet. I sat and looked at it for a while. I could feel myself shaking. A lovely nurse reassured me that I would be okay. She told me that it was a very low dose and that I was in hospital so if I did have a bad reaction, I was in the best place. With a very shaky hand, I took it. I woke up the next morning perfectly fine. My hands had a slight tremor, which is apparently normal, but it subsided after a few hours.

I was then introduced to the group programme. My mouth dropped when I saw the number of groups. It was a whole-day programme somewhat resembling a school time table. At first, I didn't go to them all. I started with just one or two a day – if I could face it.

The focus was group therapy, which terrified me. There was also art therapy, which intrigued me, and then there were mindfulness groups, and various other sessions. I thought that I would never take to those group therapy sessions. How could I possibly talk about my issues in front of all these people? I watched as others opened up so easily.

Looking back, the group programme was *incredible*. It was so far removed from anything else I had done in any hospital. One particular group, run by a male therapist, was intense. He had a way of getting things out of people; a way of making people realise things that maybe they didn't want to realise. On my first session with him, I went as red as a beet when he probed me. I wanted the ground to swallow me up. I dreaded his groups initially, but after a while, I came to look forward to them.

I made some more good friends in that group too. We all joked that even if you went into his group without dad issues, you'd come out with them, because the sessions always seemed to be father-focussed. I think that actually a lot of us did have father issues, and he got them out of us.

Some of those groups were very triggering. He made me think about things that I didn't want to think about. In one session, I ended up opening up about my dad. He pushed for more: how I felt, what I really thought. I came out of that room on the verge of a panic attack. I thought he was a dickhead for doing that to me, but actually, he was a really nice bloke with the knack for pushing people's boundaries, which isn't a bad thing. It hurts like hell, but I got a lot from his groups, and I believe that he is extremely good at his job.

All the other group sessions were about sharing feelings more generally. In art therapy, we would be given a theme and then let loose to create something. We would sit in a circle at the end of the session and talk about our creations. It was amazing to see how it worked. At the end, you would see people making realisations about their creations, even though they weren't aware they were doing it at the time.

In these groups, especially as there were so many of them, I heard many stories. *So many different journeys and battles.* A lot of them made me cry. One girl in particular was so against sharing, but then she gave the most heart-wrenching story. I thought about how incredibly brave she was. I wanted so much to give her a hug, but I knew she wouldn't have wanted that.

Everyone's stories were so different. They were heart-breaking, but we all had one thing in common: we suffered from mental health issues. The stories may have been different, we came from different backgrounds and we had different lives, but we were all here because we had come to a crisis point in one way or another.

It's amazing the strength and support patients can give each other and how we all felt united by those groups. I really wish that other hospitals would have that sort of programme. It can be so incredibly powerful. Ultimately, this is what led to the huge progress I made while in the Nightingale hospital, and after.

One day, I came across a girl having a cigarette. I felt a little intimidated to talk to her; I thought she looked like one of those people you see in films, from rough London streets. She said hi to me and asked me why I was there. I told her and asked her the same. She told me she had a heroin addiction, which I had kind of guessed. She said that she wanted to go home. She was scared and actually very timid. I gave her some encouragement, and when I left she looked at me and said, 'thank you so much for talking to me and being kind to me.' I smiled at her and as I turned away my eyes filled with tears. I reminded myself that you should never judge a book by its cover. Every time I saw her after that, I made sure that I spoke to her and asked her how she was doing. I really liked her, and I pray that she got the help she needed.

The lithium dose was slowly increased and, little by little, my hope was restored. I went to more and more groups. I saw the psychiatrist regularly, who I thought was just the most wonderful lady that I had ever met. It didn't matter what I told her, she didn't bat an eyelid – it was like water off a duck's back. When I told her what a terrible mother I was, she was kind and told me why this wasn't the case.

She spoke to me about bipolar disorder. She suggested that we make a list of my warning signs, so I was aware in the future when something may be brewing. I was tormented over the manic episode. The flashbacks would panic me. I felt ridiculous. I didn't even believe in god and yet I'd had all these intense religious thoughts and feelings. I desperately struggled with feeling that I was just a total lunatic. The psychiatrist would explain to me that it was quite common, but I couldn't get past it.

One day, I bit the bullet and even though I wished the ground would swallow me up, I handed her the scribbled notes I had made during my last manic episode. I needed to do it so that she could see what had been going on in my head at the time, rather me trying to explain it. When I talked about it, I just wanted to shut down. I wanted her to confirm whether I was just crazy or not.

The wait until I next saw her was awful. I thought she was just going to say that I was crazy. She would tell me that it wasn't bipolar, I was, in fact, just beyond help, and like all the other doctors before her, she was going to let me down.

She didn't. She simply handed me back the pages and said that it was quite common for bipolar disorder. It wasn't anything she hadn't seen before. I wanted to hug her. I had never experienced this before. It was like I was waiting for her to trip up, to say something that wasn't very nice, but she never did.

Other patients started to mention how I looked like a different person than when I came in. I started to feel it. I was still having difficulty processing what had happened, but I also felt a sense of calm. The lithium was totally different to any other medication I had tried. I still felt embarrassed that I was taking it, but with the help of the groups and the psychiatrist, I realised that I shouldn't be. It was stigma and nothing more. At the end of the day, if it helped get me better, then it really didn't matter what it was!

I left the hospital after four weeks. I thanked everyone for their help. I told the psychiatrist a million times how incredibly grateful to her I was. It was agreed that I would see her every three months outpatient.

When I returned home, I felt a sense of peace that I hadn't felt in a long time. Chris agrees that, unlike the admission the previous year, I came home like a different person. I was able to relax, to process things easier, and just generally live as a better functioning human being.

I carried on seeing Rebecca. When I first saw her, she gave me a huge hug. She even apologised for not being able to do more at that time; she knew I needed a hospital admission but that her hands had been tied. Of course, I told her that she had nothing to be sorry for. I was immensely grateful to her, she had gone above and beyond, and I will never forget it. She said that at least now she had seen me during a manic episode, so it would never be disputed again. She was right, and I was grateful at least that it had been her that witnessed it. I knew it had upset her, and she admitted that it had. That just shows how kind she was and how much she genuinely cared.

Unfortunately, my sessions with her came to an end about a year later. She said that she had had been dreading it, but that she was moving on to a new job. We both got upset and I hugged her. We had almost become friends, it wasn't like seeing a therapist in a formal sense anymore. I was gutted. I knew that this was her career and that it was what it was, but there are still times that I miss her tremendously.

As it turned out, not long after Chris got made redundant and so the healthcare stopped, and I wouldn't have been able to see her any longer anyway. Chris got redundancy pay but he was having no luck finding another job. That was a stressful time and really put to the test how well I could cope!

I told the Nightingale psychiatrist when I next saw her. I was terrified of being thrown back into NHS services. I couldn't bear the thought of it. She told me that if I could afford to, she would still see me every three months at a reduced rate. I could have kissed her. I felt totally safe under her care. I could text her or Chris could telephone her if there was a problem. I couldn't bear the thought of losing this wonderful woman when I'd only just found her. So that's what was agreed to. I seriously cannot thank this psychiatrist enough for simply being a good egg and treating me the way that she did, and still continues to do.

I carried on having flashbacks from the manic episode. I lived in fear that it was going to happen again. For a while, I was on high alert. I had struggled with my moods for so long that it was like I was waiting for it to find me, but when it did, it was more like it just peeked around the corner or brushed shoulders with me, rather than grabbing me full throttle around the throat. Even with Chris' redundancy, aside from some minor peaks and troughs, I remained stable.

I started to gain hope. A hope that had been a long time lost. I started to think that maybe, just maybe, it wasn't me. *I wasn't crazy.* I had just been ill and never received the correct help.

I felt somewhat resentful that it had taken all these years, all this heartache, to find a doctor that would simply sit and listen, and, quite frankly, do their job as it should be done. I was also grateful. I was grateful that I got to experience the help that I had. It was only possible for a short time, while Chris had that job. They say everything happens for a reason.

SEMICOLON

I sit writing this, reflecting on all these years past and the battle I have fought. I say *fought,* but the reality is that I am still fighting. Nearly every day, to some degree, I fight. Mental illness doesn't disappear. Even with the best medication and the best doctors, I'm not sure that it's possible to be 100% recovered.

However, as I sit beside my daughter, engrossed in the videos on her phone (with the song 'London bridge is falling down' on repeat, driving me slightly demented) I realise how far I've come. Is everything perfect? *Of course not.* Life isn't perfect. Perfect is unachievable. I still struggle with this and my perfectionism grinds me down, but I am learning to manage the thoughts.

I guess the big question is: would I change everything if I could? I'm not sure. The answer to this would be different at different times of my life. During bad periods, I'm sure I would say that I would change everything. I would say that I'm sick of the struggles and the depression that still hits me can be devastating. But on the whole, I feel like my experiences have made me who I am. Because of them, I think the way I do, I hold kindness close and I am more open-minded and empathetic. I am more resilient too. Not only to moods and mental health, but I have more general resilience to ride out negative situations, knowing that they too will eventually pass, no matter how hard they seem.

I am not perfect. I am not immune to falling again. Nor am I totally recovered – that is unrealistic. I am stronger. I am much better equipped to deal with myself, my moods, and my mind.

I believe that there are some positives things to come from having a mental illness. It makes you strong. It gives you more of an awareness and less of a tunnel-vision view on life. For me, the main positive to come from all of my negative experiences, all of the fights and the years of getting nowhere, is that it has given me passion. I have a huge passion to help others, to raise awareness and reduce stigma. I love this passion. It keeps me fighting. It lights a fire in my belly, and it's something that I would never have had if I had not gone through all the things that I have gone through. I finally feel like I have a purpose. *All that I have been through has been for something.* Because of this, I'm not sure that I'd change anything. My life is my life. If I changed it, I wouldn't be me. I've fought hard for me.

Perception counts for a lot. How we think can have a huge impact on how we function. I used to be very angry at people, at the fact that I have mental health issues, that I never trained in a career, that things hadn't gone how I wanted them to. This way of thinking becomes like a habit. It keeps you down; each day becomes about how you are or are not feeling, rather than just living. Sometimes I look at people's social media and recognise this way of thinking and behaviour. It's so easy to get trapped in that cycle. When you have suffered with mental illness for so long, you can almost become it.

The last thing that my therapist Rebecca said to me has really stayed with me. As I walked out the room she said, *'Katie, just live.'*

I never say that I *am* bipolar, I say that I *have* bipolar. I am not bipolar, I am Katie, and I have an illness that is, in some ways, a large part of my life, but it is only a small part of *me*. That one realisation can make a big difference.

It can actually be scary to think that way. It's been a huge part of your life and you lose yourself at times. It can be hard to get back your identity, your true self, but the true you is still in there, and you can find it. Just give yourself time.

I have a small handmade business on Esty: www.etsy.com/shop/katiescabinhandmade (shameless plug, I know). I often feel my perfectionism creeping into my business. The amount of times I have thought that something is rubbish, only to get a five-star review from a customer who is beyond happy. Each time that happens, I make a mental note of it. This has helped me to deal with future thoughts and behaviours – I can remind myself that it's my mind playing tricks on me.

When I get an order, I sometimes feel the need to complete it immediately, even if the processing time is two–three weeks. When I have a lot of orders at the same time, it can tip my mind into chaos and frustration. I am learning to take a step back and evaluate what is going on in reality – not just in my perfectionist mind. Sometimes I succeed, sometimes I don't and I have a bit of a meltdown, but that's okay.

For so long, this is how I've been wired; it's not just going to vanish. It's something I have to live with, to constantly remind myself of, and to fight, but that's okay too. It's a constant learning curve. I have to retrain my mind to think differently, which is a daily process.

What about my anorexia – am I totally recovered? I don't think anyone ever can be. I can say that I am recovered because I live my life and I eat without tormenting myself. Unfortunately, over the years, I have ended up with some physical health conditions that I wonder whether are a result of anorexia. One of them is chronic IBS, to the point that my diet is very plain and boring, consisting of a small food group. Oh, the irony that I would love a big fat pizza or a hamburger now, but I actually can't.

There are still times that I 'feel fat' and it preoccupies my mind. I find myself looking in the bathroom mirror at my stomach more than I should. I feel a bit crappy eating food, and I hear that voice whisper gently in my ear. It never lasts long and, knock on wood, I have not given in to any of those behaviours for eight years now. For that, I am both proud and grateful, because I have seen people that I was in the hospital with still struggling to this day.

I was determined that anorexia wouldn't beat me, and I am proud to say that it hasn't. It may brush past my shoulder from time to time, but I don't let it in. I know that I couldn't go back to that. I wouldn't want to go back to that. Plus, I like my chocolate and biscuits far too much now. There's no way I'm giving those bad boys up.

Seriously though, I'm a long time into my anorexia recovery now. I have a good understanding of how it works – enough to recognise when it creeps back in to my mind and to deal with it.

To anyone out there still struggling with anorexia I would say this:

As you're reading this, I know it may feel like you can never get here. You've tried, and it's not working. You can't get rid of that voice in your head. The compulsion to restrict, purge, whatever it may be, is too strong for you to resist. I understand. I understand that feeling 100 percent, and it's awful. It feels like you will never have a normal life. You will never stop worrying about food, and you will never stop feeling guilty about eating it. All these stories of recovery make you think, 'good for them.' Maybe you even feel a pang of hope. But then, as you put down the book, you are flung back into the real world and those consuming thoughts. I know because I was you. I was doing what you are doing and thinking what you are thinking. I read a book like this one and thought, 'that will never be me.' I also know that no matter how much someone tells you that it can be you, you don't quite believe them. Whatever I say here, if you're in the grips of anorexia, you won't truly believe it because that other voice in your head is too strong. Just for this moment, tell it to shut up. Tell it that it may, just may, be wrong, because here is someone else who was also told the same things and now is free from that grip. I eat what I want (within reason, because of my delicate tummy). I eat when I want. From time to time, I get a small repercussion, but it doesn't overpower me. You can do this too. It is possible. It is within grasp. I'm not going to say that it's easy, and it doesn't happen overnight – there's no magic 'poof' and it's all better, but over time, slowly, small step by small step, it gets better. The little things become big things and the big things become the norm. That's where we all want to be, right? The bog-standard norm that throws us a curveball from time to time; sometimes we dodge it, sometimes we fall, but we get back up, we carry on fighting in the normal day-to-day. You will get to your normal day-to-day. You just have to keep fighting. Most importantly, you have to want it. I understand that sometimes it's not the right time to want it; that is usually when the reasons behind the anorexia are too strong. Figuring out the reasons for your anorexia is crucial. These reasons are its backbone and what gives it its power. Once you know those reasons (and that is hard to deal with) the anorexia loses some of its grasp. There, you will find the will to fight. So, keep talking. Keep being honest with yourself. Don't shut people out. It's so important to be honest. In doing so, you take some of anorexia's power away and finally you will be able to tackle it head on. You've got this! Don't ever, ever lose hope.

What about my moods – am I recovered from bipolar? As much as I wish this were possible, it's not. There isn't a cure for bipolar. It's been hard to deal with the fact that this is going to be a permanent figure in my life. It comes along and messes with my moods like some kind of intruder.

I still see my psychiatrist every three months at the Nightingale hospital, and I still take lithium and quetiapine. Sometimes I resent it, usually when I've got the flu or another illness and can't take ibuprofen because of how it interacts with lithium. Sometimes I wish I didn't have bipolar, but other times I am thankful, because it has made me who I am.

I can be fine for some time and then I will feel myself getting a little jittery, get too involved in my crafts and get so many ideas that there isn't enough hours in the day to do them all. This will then fizzle out and inevitably leave me feeling low. I will completely lose interest in something that just a few days before I was excited about. It can make life very confusing. Sometimes I question whether I am genuinely passionate about something, or whether it is just another fleeting moment, but I'm learning that I can't question myself for every move I make. Of course, I find the periods where I lose interest hard.

I'm a naturally creative person and someone who likes to be 'doing.' I rarely sit still until the evening – and that's the way I like it. Is this partly the bipolar? I don't know. Maybe, but it's at a level that I like. I like to be thinking, doing, creating. When this stops, and the depression takes over for a while, it takes all my might not to succumb and sink into the feeling that I have no purpose. In these times, my wonderful partner Chris has to take over some. He fetches our daughter from school and helps with many of the things I would usually do. I hate these times, but I am starting to accept that this is okay. I have bipolar disorder, and this will happen. Granted, I don't always accept it very well at the time. The big difference now is that I have been through it so many times. I now not only know and accept that it will it happen, but also that it will pass; as quickly as it comes over me, it will wash away again. Sometimes it's hard to hold on to this. Sometimes I feel the suicidal thoughts creeping into my mind, but I bat them away more successfully now, knowing that this too shall pass.

I can't take all the credit; the lithium has helped greatly. The constant blood tests are a bit of a ball ache, and it has screwed with my thyroid. My psychiatrist and I are constantly battling to find the right balance between a therapeutic lithium dose and a healthy thyroid. However, even if it's not perfect, it is so much better with the lithium that without. Now I only touch hypomania and depression before it fizzles out (up until now at least, fingers crossed). I have to be honest and say that touching hypomania is not always a bad thing! Yes, sometimes I panic as I feel it getting to be a bit too much, but most of the time it gives me lots of new ideas and energy (some of those ideas may come to me at 2.00 am, but hey ho!)

I won't lie, I get scared that it may not just fizzle out. While I have a wonderful psychiatrist, I no longer have private health care, so I would be back under the care of the crisis team and NHS services. This terrifies me to my bones. It's sad that this is the case. We are lucky to have the NHS. It's just unfortunate that, apart from some experiences at the eating disorder unit, I cannot say that I have had positive experiences with it. However, I also know that I cannot live in this fear.

I try to take each day as it comes. It can be challenging, especially as, over the years, I've also accrued some physical health problems to deal with, but I am always grateful that I no longer live in that constant awful swing of moods, the grip of anorexia, and that I have people around me who care – even if it is a small circle. I am grateful to be where I am, in comparison to back then.

I love my little girl to the moon and back. She is my world. I am a protective mother, but I think that is understandable. She is confident, extremely sensitive, and already has said some things that have made me wonder whether she has inherited some of my traits. Such as, she told me that she 'checks her things' before she goes to sleep. I know she hasn't learned this from me as my own checking procedure these days is very minimal and reduced to a single box of items that I check once a week before I go to bed, and she is sound asleep. Unfortunately, this sort of obsessive behaviour runs in my mum's side of the family. When she said that, my heart sunk a little. She's so young. On the other hand, I am well prepared for it. I know what to look out for, and we are incredibly close. She tells me I am her best friend, which always makes my heart glow. I vow to bring her up so that she feels like she can always talk to me, and if she ever has any issues, I vow to be right by her side. She will never go through anything alone. In a way I'm glad that I grew up how I did, because over my dead body will my little girl ever experience the same.

I probably go a little over the top; I praise every single picture that she shows me. I also have, not a memory box, but a memory suitcase of her baby things and separate boxes of pictures. Chris jokes that by the time she leaves home, and we supposedly give her these memories, she will need an extra van and room. I know it's a little excessive, but I guess it's a desire for her to have happy memories, for her to see that I adored her, and I loved her to the ends of the earth.

My little dog Alfie saved my life more times that his little furry face even realises. The amount of times I've gotten myself well for this little man is unreal. He's my second baby (well, my first, technically). Everyone comments on how much I love my dog, and I do. He's not a dog to me, he's my family, my best friend, and I love him to the stars and back. He licks my tears and lies with me if I'm not doing well. He's like my left arm. I'd be lost without him.

Then there's Chris. *Pain in the arse that he is!* I'm kidding. He has been my saviour. From the days before we got together, when he looked after me and made sure I was okay, to going for a stroll in his socks due to the shear stress of my mania and dealing with it all on his own. He has never given up on me. I tell you now, he has put up with more from me than a lot of blokes would put up with in a lifetime. He really is my hero. That sounds cheesy, but I would never have made it without him. He continues to put up with my mini meltdowns and funny ways. He accepts it. He does what he can and always tries to say the right thing. He's fought for me on so many occasions and put up with a lot. When I was in the eating disorder unit, he came every single night after work and got home at god knows what time to do it all again the next day. I'll never forget the one day that he couldn't come, he felt like the worst person in the world. I couldn't believe it, after what I had been used to. He is a diamond. Yes, we have the same niggles and rows, as any couple does. He gets fed up with my moods and I get fed up with how he's so laid back he's almost horizontal sometimes. They say opposites attract. We bounce along together and honestly, he keeps me calm and on a normal level when sometimes I struggle to myself.

You see, 'recovery' is different for everyone. It means different things to different people. The truth of the matter is that it's never perfect. It's not plain sailing. Especially with mental illness. It's a battle, but it's a battle I am determined to keep fighting, and to do my dammed best to keep winning.

I'm under no illusion that there will never come a time that it will once again over power me. Until that day, I will keep fighting the very best I can. *So can you.* That's all we can do.

I no longer speak to my dad. I haven't done so since that day that I told him he could come over and then never heard from him again. Do I miss him? Of course, I tend to get a bit emotional over father and daughter scenes in films, where a dad tells his daughter that he is proud of her. It's hard not to. I wish I had that relationship, but I also know that I can't. I have often beaten myself up over whether he is ill and actually believes what he says. I am unsure, but I stick to the fact that he never opened up to me, he was never honest, so there is not much I can do. I cannot have that sort of toxic relationship in my life, and certainly not around my little girl. It hurts. It really does. Especially when I think about what he must have told other people about me to get them to believe his stories, but when it boils down to it, is not worth it. It's not worth the effect it had on my mind. I can't deal with that sort of relationship in my life. Especially not now that I have come so far. I often think 'maybe he's changed,' but I highly doubt it. I just have to accept that's how it is. I have had an up and down relationship with my Mom and much of the same is true. I have just realised that I have to accept what I cannot change and change what I can to make my own life happier. That is all any of us can do.

Unfortunately, I have been unable to work full time because of the mental and physical health issues. This has always killed me inside. I worked so hard at school and worked after leaving school. It's been hard to accept, but so much has happened over the years, it's taken an awful long time to be able to function, let alone to train in a career or go to university. My priority has been my sanity!

My dream is to train as a counsellor which I have recently embarked on. My ultimate dream is to have a charity one day – a retreat for people who are feeling suicidal who do not have access to services.

My own handmade business has been very good for me and uses my creative talents. Creativity is so useful in mental health issues. It helps to focus the mind. In bad times, if I can get myself to do one little creative thing, I will feel a tiny bit better.

I always hoped that one day, all of my suffering and mental illness experiences will have been for something. Mostly, I doubted that it would, but there was always a small part of me that thought one day, maybe, I could use it for something good. I had wanted to study mental health nursing all those years ago, but that never worked out. For a long time, I have had it in my mind to train as a counsellor. I have started that training now and will see where that takes me. Not only that, but without me planning for it, I have started campaigning on mental health issues – which I am extremely passionate about.

I love sending my Esty orders out in pretty packaging with hand-made shiny stickers. I love to think that they make people smile, even before they've opened the parcel. One day, I looked at these stickers and thought that I could send people struggling with mental health issues free 'Happy Post.' I set up a website where people could send me requests for happy post if they are having a tough time or know sometime who is. I also set up an area to blog and vlog about my experiences and mental health in general, with the aim of making people feel less alone and to know that it's okay to speak openly about feelings and experiences.

Following the 'Happy Post' I decided to start a new project 'notes of hope'. I hand wrote 150 notes and hung them along a bridge known for people ending their lives. The notes were inspirational quotes and messages. Most came from my heart. I hoped to reach someone else in their most hopeless moment, based on my own experiences with feeling suicidal. Sadly, the council ripped them down, deeming them to be a 'distraction to motorists.' It was a high pedestrian bridge that from the road below the notes merely looked like distant black squares – barely visible. This was picked up by the media and shared by various radio stations, ITV Central online, local newspapers and RT News. I started a campaign to get them rehung and from there, things grew.

I started doing some vlogs for *Time to change* – a social movement, working to change the way with think and act about mental health problems. I had interviews with radio stations about mental health and suicide awareness, and was also interviewed on the BBC Victoria Derbyshire Show about self-harm statistics for teenage girls. I got involved with other people's mental health projects, and went on to do more of my own, which were amazingly well received. I finally felt like I belonged somewhere with a purpose.

Most recently, at the time of writing, I have done a photo shoot as part of the Lloyds Bank #GetTheInsideOut Campaign. I have more projects of my own lined up to raise awareness for mental health. I am loving every second. It finally feels that my life has been leading to something, that maybe it was all meant to be.

I am finally free. I am totally honest about my mental health, my experiences, and my life. I can finally talk about it with pride rather than dodging the issue. It is no longer swept under a rug. In fact, I welcome talking about it openly and very much hope to carry on raising awareness and building my platform as a campaigner.

I am extremely passionate about doing this, and I really hope to use my voice as a positive influence and to show others that the seemingly impossibility of making it through mental illness is entirely possible. It's not quick, and it's not simple, but it is possible. As one of my favorite quotes says: 'don't be ashamed of your story, one day it will inspire others.'

In my normal day-to-day life, with my little family, I am happy. That's all I ever wanted. I am still learning, but I am anorexia free (aside from fleeting moments), and my moods are so much more under control. I am OCD free, apart from my weekly check (although if Chris goes away for the night, this does gear up a level). My anxiety only rears its head occasionally. So, I think I can say I am in recovery as much as one with a mental health condition can be in recovery. It's managed, and that's the very best I can ask for.

I find crafts, hobbies, and music to be powerful. I think it's a great thing to have songs that you know will lift your mood, as well as those that make you think when reflection is necessary, because sometimes it is. I have songs for every mood. I love a bit of Eminem, I love the big divas like Whitney and Mariah, I adore Emeli Sande, Adele, Sam Smith. My 'theme tune' is Beyonce's 'Listen.' It doesn't matter how many times I listen to that song, it makes the hairs on my arms stand up because it relates so much to my life and my story. Emeli Sande's 'Read all about it' also resonates with me and I have listened to it a lot while writing this book.

I have pictures with quotes, a quote a day calendar, all these things I find helpful.

It's about finding the things that work for you. I also have numerous rings with quotes on them. One says, 'She believed she could, so she did.' Another says, 'Strive for progress not perfection.' Another says, 'This too shall pass,' with a semi colon. There was actually a semicolon movement surrounding mental health. It was for those people who have been suicidal and survived; the semicolon signifies 'my story hasn't ended.'

My story hasn't ended. It will continue and, I hope, on an onward and upward path, but I feel more prepared for whichever path it takes.

We all need to stick together, to keep speaking out. At times I've been terrified about writing this book. Who might see it, who won't believe me, what will people think? But, you know what? It's my story. Going right back to that poem that I did for my college audition: this is my truth. My experiences, and my version of events. If other people don't like it, then I can't help that. I struggled all those years, and the most important thing to me is that I put that to good use and possibly give others some hope.

You've got this. Find your theme tune, play it at the highest possible decibel, keep fighting, and always finish with a semicolon;

AFTERWORD

I want to share a little bit of "Happy Post" with anyone that feels hopeless as I did. This is for you:

Dear YOU,

You are having a bad day, so much so that you have struggled to function, maybe even struggled to get out of bed.

Please know that this isn't the forever you. It isn't the true you. It's just the for now you.

The true you is still in there. I know you think that they've gone, that you've lost them. You haven't.

The true you is just a little lost. It's taken the wrong turning down a dark road and is struggling to see its way back. This doesn't mean that it is lost forever.

It is working super hard to make its way back to you again, to help make you feel whole. It's tiring work and so it is having to rest along the way, as should you.

The truth is that you are both working super hard. You're both very tired and so in this period it is okay to rest. It's okay to feel lost and it's okay to feel how you do, as long as you hold on and keep going because I promise you, the true you will be back ... And it may just be closer than you think.

Never lose hope, even if it is a small thread that is frayed, hope is more powerful than you think and it holds all the fight that you need. Stay strong.

Katie

x

23271177R00215

Printed in Great Britain
by Amazon